Staffing the Principalship

FINDING, COACHING, AND MENTORING SCHOOL LEADERS

Suzette Lovely

Association for Supervision
and Curriculum Development
Alexandria, Virginia USA

Association for Supervision and Curriculum Development
1703 N. Beauregard St.• Alexandria, VA 22311-1714 USA
Telephone: 800-933-2723 or 703-578-9600 • Fax: 703-575-5400
Web site: http://www.ascd.org • E-mail: member@ascd.org

Gene R. Carter, *Executive Director;* Nancy Modrak, *Director of Publishing;* Julie Houtz, *Director of Book Editing & Production;* Darcie Russell, *Project Manager;* Georgia McDonald, *Senior Graphic Designer;* Valerie Sprague, *Desktop Publishing Specialist;* Dina Seamon, *Production Specialist*

All Web links in this book are correct as of the publication date below but may have become inactive or otherwise modified since that time. If you notice a deactivated or changed link, please e-mail books@ascd.org with the words "Link Update" in the subject line. In your message, please specify the Web link, the book title, and the page number on which the link appears.

Printed in the United States of America.

ISBN: 0-87120-834-2   ASCD product no.: 104010
ASCD member price: $20.95   nonmember price: $25.95   s1/04

e-books ($25.95) • netLibrary ISBN 087120-966-7 • ebrary 0-87120-967-5

Library of Congress Cataloging-in-Publication Data

Lovely, Suzette, 1958–
  Staffing the principalship : finding, coaching, and mentoring school leaders / Suzette Lovely.
      p. cm.
Includes bibliographical references and index.
  ISBN 0-87120-834-2 (alk. paper)
  1. School principals—In-service training—United States. 2. School principals—Recruiting—United States. 3. School principals—Job satisfaction—United States. 4. Mentoring in education—United States. I. Association for Supervision and Curriculum Development. II. Title.
  LB2831.93.L68 2004
  371.2′012′0973—dc22

                                                        2003024246

13 12 11 10 09 08 07 06 05 04   12 11 10 9 8 7 6 5 4 3 2 1

Staffing the Principalship

FINDING, COACHING,
AND MENTORING SCHOOL LEADERS

1

Understanding What the Principal Shortage Means for Your District

I'm really worried about the crisis. If we continue to burn out these people, we're not going to find leaders.

—Glen "Max" McGee, Illinois State School Superintendent
from Dell'Angela (2001), p. 3.

According to the Educational Research Service (ERS, 1999), nearly 40 percent of all public school principals will retire or leave the position for other reasons before 2010. The Bureau of Labor Statistics anticipates the number of available jobs in school administration will grow 10 to 20 percent over the next five years (Institute for Educational Leadership [IEL], 2000, p. 3). Considering there are roughly 93,000 principalships nationwide (IEL, 2000), the vacancy rate in the United States could soar exponentially.

With the average age of a principal being 50 years or older, compounded by fewer people pursuing advancement opportunities leading to a principalship, many districts are scrambling to find strong leaders (ERS, 2000). The elementary principalship alone has experienced a 42 percent turnover rate since 1988. Attrition is expected to remain constant for the next several years. With such significant losses, it should come as no surprise that the greatest deficit of principals is at the high school level.

What does the available pool look like? During the late 1970s, an urban school district could expect as many as 40 applicants for every principal opening (Olson, 1999). Today that average is a mere 10. Nearly half of the 1,100 public schools in New York City are managed by principals with less than three years experience (Archer, 2002b). In 2002–2003, the state of Washington summoned 34 retired principals back to work to fill in as districts desperately sought new prospects (Association of Washington School Principals, 2003). Although women constitute 35 percent of the nation's principals, up from 2 percent in 1988, there's been only a 3 percent increase in the number of minority principals since 1999 (Fenwick & Collins Pierce, 2001). In an era of rising minority student enrollments, this statistic is another cause for concern.

In July 2001, the *Los Angeles Times* reported that California was producing 2,000 to 3,500 newly licensed administrators each year, yet only 38 percent actually assume leadership positions in California schools (Orozco & Oliver, 2001). Most opt to remain in the classroom or change careers entirely. No other profession can claim such staggering disinterest after a trainee's preparation. To make matters worse, a study published by the Association of California School Administrators (ACSA, 2000) disclosed that just 7 percent of the state's superintendents view principal preparation programs as "excellent." Nearly one-fourth of these superintendents described the preparation of existing candidates as "inadequate." Despite these worries, only about 3 in 10 California school districts offer any formal mentoring programs for new principals. At the national level, only 27 percent of reporting districts say they have programs in place to recruit or prepare aspiring principals (IEL, 2000). It appears the applicants under consideration aren't qualified to deal with the complexities of the job, and most districts have no immediate plans to expand their applicant pool.

Many factors drive people away from the principalship. Principals are being asked to do more with less time and fewer resources. The expectations placed on principals by state and local policymakers, parents, and the public have reached epic heights. Gerald Tirozzi, the executive director of the National Association of Secondary School Principals (NASSP), bemoans the conflicting paradox that haunts high school principals. Tirozzi says that though principals face greater accountability, they've been stripped of authority or autonomy at the school level (Stricherz, 2001). As a result, the entire notion of learning leadership is thrown out the window as other less important issues take precedence. Consider my two dearest high school principal friends as examples. Rarely do they have time for a Friday night movie or a Sunday shopping spree. If they're not at the football game or winter formal, they're performing air guitar or enjoying a delicious chicken dinner at the water polo banquet.

What's Driving People Away from the Principalship?

Since the mid-1990s, an abundance of research has been conducted to ascertain what's keeping people away from the principalship and what's causing them to leave the job once they have it. In study after study, a lethal mixture of the following deterrents has transcended every level and demographic group of principals: time and overload, increasing responsibilities, work-related stress, salary, and institutional interference.

Time and Overload

Long Hours: A principal works upward of 54 to 80 hours each week, including evenings and weekends (ERS, 2000; Yerkes & Guaglianone, 1998). This is a taxing schedule for even the most energetic individual. One Illinois high school principal lamented, "No matter how visible you are, you are not visible enough" (Dell'Angela, 2001, p. 5).

Too Much on the Principal's Plate: Few duties fall outside the scope of a principal's job description. When one task is complete, two more are added to the plate. A recurrence of problems and hastily planned initiatives make it impossible for principals to get ahead. As the "to do" list grows, other responsibilities are not taken away.

Increasing Responsibilities

Government Mandates and Accountability: Nearly every lawmaker wants to be dubbed the education czar. New laws and requirements at the state and federal level are being passed in record number—often with little foresight or adequate funding. High school exit exams, state testing programs, class-size reduction, teacher induction and credentialing, and the No Child Left Behind Act are just a few examples.

Societal Problems Reflected in Student Populations: School safety, drug use, teen pregnancy, and teen suicide scratch the surface of what a principal must cope with. Additionally, schools are being asked to provide day care and other health-related services on their campuses, thus creating more programs for the principal to oversee.

Work-Related Stress

Meeting Achievement Standards: Whether a school is low or high performing, demands for improvement are equally weighted for principals. Keeping abreast of ever-changing curricula and teaching methods further adds to the stress experienced by principals.

Special Education Requirements: Parental demands for expanding services, changing Individuals with Disabilities Education Act (IDEA) mandates, full inclusion, Section 504 accommodations, and daylong meetings are just a few of the special education challenges that today's principals face. Lawyers and advocates are commonplace in individualized education plan (IEP) meetings and hearings, adding intimidation and stress to the workload.

School Funding Issues: Managing hard-to-understand budgets, dealing with yearly shortfalls, losing support staff because of inadequate funding, and overseeing fund-raising activities to support extra programs requires fiscal savvy. Most principals describe this as their weakest area of school management (Alvy & Robbins, 1998; Ruenzel, 1998).

Salary

Little Financial Incentive to Become a Principal: On average, the daily rate of pay for a new assistant principal is barely 5 percent more than that of an experienced teacher (Archer, 2002a). In addition, principals generally work 11 months of the year, whereas teachers generally work 9 months of the year. There is little incentive for senior teachers to leave the classroom.

Inadequate Pay: The per diem rate for principals isn't commensurate with the managerial responsibilities of their position as gauged by looking at the salaries of professionals with similar levels of responsibility (ERS, 2000). Salaries have not kept pace with the demands of the job.

Institutional Interference

Inability to Fire Poor Teachers: Principals feel their hands are tied when it comes to releasing ineffective teachers. The process of teacher dismissal is so cumbersome, few principals are willing to take it on (Johnson, 2002).

Negotiated Agreements: Constraints in employee contracts often preclude principals from making rapid change and moving schools forward (Johnson, 2002). For instance, school-based management and shared decision-making provisions in many collective bargaining agreements require hours of discussion to implement a single idea. With a high school faculty of 120, it might take an entire year of bartering to institute a 30-minute tutorial period. Most principals simply run out of steam before consensus is ever reached.

Stymied by the Central Office: Principals often view the bureaucratic and political structures of the central office as a major obstacle (New Teacher Center, 2002). Excessive paperwork, unrealistic deadlines, unfocused staff development efforts, and mandates unrelated to improving student achievement are a few of the issues principals must contend with.

By understanding the conditions that discourage candidates from seeking the principalship, districts can begin to examine the internal systems that may contribute to an already depleted pool. Central office staff and site-based leadership teams should look for quick and simple fixes to make the principalship more attractive. For example, although raising salaries may be impossible, a district can minimize the number of meetings for which principals are called away from their work sites. A simple gesture of dispatching a special education administrator to help a principal facilitate a difficult IEP meeting can also go a long way. Easing attendance requirements at school and district events is also helpful. Finally, to introduce the practice of selective abandonment, the superintendent might conduct a brainstorming session with principals to determine which duties are essential. Otherwise, principals never really know which tasks are politically acceptable to let go. Too often the central office is blinded by its own agenda and fails to recognize that changing the culture downtown can significantly change the outcome uptown. Making some relatively easy adjustments to age-old practices minimizes the burnout of existing principals and can make the job more attractive to newcomers.

A New Paradigm of Leadership

I work upward of 70 hours per week, including evenings and weekends. Today I disaggregated test data, searched the trash dumpster for a lost retainer, spoke at a Chamber of Commerce breakfast, developed a spending plan for a $500,000 grant, counseled a distraught parent about her daughter's proclivity toward body piercing, and met with officials from the nuclear power plant to discuss potassium iodide distribution in the event of a terrorist attack. Who am I? Why a middle school principal, of course!

Contemporary principals look and act much differently than the ones we remember from our school days. One minute the job demands intellectual savvy; the next minute it calls for an iron-clad stomach and a durable pair of latex gloves. According to Richard DuFour, retired superintendent of the acclaimed Adlai Stevenson High School in Lincolnshire, Illinois, and nationally recognized author and consultant, today's principals must "have a sense of urgency, balanced by the patience to sustain [the school] for the long haul." He continues, "They must focus on the future, but remain grounded in today. They must see the big picture, while maintaining a close [eye] on the details. [And] they must be strong leaders who give away power to others" (DuFour, 1999, p. 12). In essence, the "benevolent dictators" of the past are being replaced by the instructional maestros of the future.

The bygone era of authoritarian and aloof school management has paved the way for the emergence of a more culturally conscious leader. For districts to compete in the domestic marketplace, deliberate efforts must be established to recruit, select, train, and inspire this new brand of principal. Several states and educational organizations have developed standards for administrative practice that define what the 21st-century principal should know and be able to do. The National Association of Elementary School Principals (NAESP, 2001), for instance, has outlined six key elements that encapsulate what is expected of this next generation of school leaders. The destiny of tomorrow's eclectic principals lies in their ability to

1. Lead their schools in a way that places student and adult learning at the center.
2. Set high expectations and standards for the academic and social development of all students and the performance of adults.
3. Demand content and instruction that ensures student achievement of agreed upon academic standards.
4. Create a culture of continuous learning for adults tied to student learning and other school goals.
5. Use multiple sources of data as tools to assess, identify, and apply instructional improvement.
6. Actively engage the community to create shared responsibility for student and school success. (NAESP, 2001, p. 2)

As the standards illustrate, modern-day principals must lead from a higher plane. Developing leadership capacity is at the core of the collaborative principal's work. Tomorrow's principals have to begin today to become learners as well as teachers. They need to exercise support rather than control. This Zen-like approach requires deep reflection and inquiry. The process of building a professional learning community cannot be left to chance. Therefore, these 21st century pioneers must meet the following demands:

- Lead through shared vision and values rather than rules and procedures.
- Enlist faculty in the decision-making process and empower individuals to act.
- Provide information, training, and parameters for staff to make good decisions.
- Be results oriented.
- Concentrate on posing the right questions rather than imposing solutions. (DuFour, 1999, p. 13–16)

Superintendents are under scrutiny to fill vacancies with candidates who fit this new paradigm of leadership. As districts look to the future, they must strive to find principals who can "orchestrate rather than dictate" (DuFour, 1999, p. 17). This effort will guarantee that our schools have the kind of leaders they so desperately need and deserve.

Can We Reinvent the Principalship?

Principal Opening in Anytown School District, USA. Qualifications: Wisdom of a sage, vision of a [chief executive officer], intellect of a scholar, leadership of a point guard, compassion of a counselor, moral strength of a nun, courage of a firefighter, craft knowledge of a surgeon, political savvy of a senator, toughness of a soldier, listening skills of a blind man, humility of a saint, collaborative skills of an entrepreneur, certitude of a civil rights activist, charisma of a stage performer, patience of Job. Salary: Lower than you might expect. (adapted from Copland, 2001, p. 528)

Although this job description clearly exaggerates what might be expected of a principal, there is no doubt that the requirements of the job have become incredibly burdensome during the last two decades. Michael Copland, assistant professor of education at Stanford University, speculates "we have reached the point where aggregate expectations for the principalship are so exorbitant, they exceed the limits of what reasonably might be expected from one person" (Copland, 2001, p. 529).

Increasing expectations have given rise to the argument that the only way to fix the problem is to reinvent the role of the principal (IEL, 2000). In essence, the job needs to be made doable. Redistributing assignments among coadministrators to reduce heavy demands on the principal's time or appointing coprincipals to lead larger schools top the list of doable suggestions (Pounder & Merrill, 2001). Another consideration is to create shared responsibility and accountability for the outcome of site decisions to redesign the principal's role.

Although these are all excellent ideas, they simply do not go far enough in addressing the systemic and cultural barriers principals have to overcome. To make the principalship truly doable would require the educational establishment to alter public opinion, lower parental expectations, eliminate political pressures, ignore diversity, and reshape our values.

A more realistic approach to reinventing the role is to teach our principals how to make time for what truly counts, because their jobs will always seem complicated and overwhelming. In his book *What's Worth Fighting For in the Principalship?*, Michael Fullan offers this poignant message to principals: "There's no point in lamenting the fact that the system is unreasonable, and no percentage in waiting around for it to become more reasonable. It won't" (Fullan, 1997, p. 5). Instead, says Fullan, we must guide principals in setting aside time for what really matters. If we teach them how to focus and prioritize, we can condition principals to become action-oriented rather than waiting for things to improve.

These sentiments appear to be echoed by principals, too. Principals generally view themselves and the complex nature of their work favorably (ERS, 2000). In fact, the majority of the principals I work with say they were drawn to the profession because they enjoy change, variety, and excitement. As leaders, I find principals to be idealistic and dedicated. Most are extremely dutiful and loyal to their district. As skilled troubleshooters, principals are keenly aware that sometimes they just need to go with the flow. It is their unwavering desire to work with students, entwined with the strong belief that they can and do positively affect many lives, that keeps a principal going (ERS, 2000; Johnson, 2002). Despite the roller-coaster ride, most principals continue to find their jobs fulfilling and would opt for the same career path again given the choice.

Completely revamping the role of the principal may be impossible, but a district can take steps to restructure the principal's duties. By assessing staffing levels and taking an honest look at the administrative responsibilities at each school site, the central office can begin to introduce support staff in stages. Hiring 10 assistant principals at once probably isn't a viable option, but there may be other support positions that can be added gradually. If districts start by establishing a well-considered plan to redistribute site leadership, principals will learn to relinquish responsibilities and decisions without the worry of sole accountability. The following positions warrant consideration:

- Program specialists who can serve several sites and cut in half the time a principal spends in IEP meetings.
- District resource teachers released from the classroom to provide various functions related to curriculum development and teacher training.
- Assistant principals split between two campuses to take on some of the instructional and managerial responsibilities.
- Deans of discipline, who cost far less than an assistant principal, to handle time-consuming discipline and other operational issues.
- An athletic director in the central office who can respond to many of the sports-related and extracurricular problems.
- A district-level investigator to research claims of sexual harassment, discrimination, worker's compensation, and other serious allegations made against or by employees, students, and parents.
- An ombudsman to mediate citizen complaints and public relations issues.

Looking at central office organization and procedures may reveal other possibilities for remodeling the principalship. Are there things that the district retains control of that can be given up? Who controls the flow of paperwork? Does anyone monitor how or when various departments communicate with principals? What "urgent" projects surface day-to-day and week-to-week that pull principals away from learning leadership? How are hiring practices structured? Do principals have any say in the selection, assignments, and transfers of teachers? Although collective bargaining agreements dictate some circumstances, there is always wiggle room. Sometimes we just need to stop, look, and listen to find it.

Finally, district administrators and principals themselves need to let go of traditions and rituals that hinder progress. When there's no one left in the building who can convince you that doing something a particular way makes sense, it's probably time to move on. Too often we find a lot of people doing the wrong things well, so we're convinced that they're right. We have to look inside ourselves to bring about the changes necessary to make schools even better. By examining our own shortcomings and challenging the status quo, leverage opportunities will surely surface. These leverage points—places where the least amount of effort spawns the greatest good—can serve as the springboard in redesigning the principal's role.

Three Approaches for Improving the Principalship

To address the burgeoning principal shortage, local districts need to tackle the problem on three fronts. First, the central office should take a long hard look at what is and isn't being done to combat the problem. Do the school board and superintendent provide leadership in designing a district recruitment plan? Do existing principals and other members of the administrative team actively participate in the recruitment process? If your district isn't experiencing a dearth of candidates, it likely will in the near future. Seeking trainable candidates and developing them from within is a sure-fire way to fill openings with leaders who best meet your district's needs.

Second, the district needs to provide practical training for new principals. Once hired, principals need intensive support and coaching. A structured orientation to the assigned school and district is a must for every first-year principal. Coaches, veteran mentors, and buddy programs should also be standard fare. The district's investment in rookie principals pays dividends in the end. In their book *If Only I Knew. . . Successful Strategies for Navigating the Principalship,* Harvey Alvy and Pam Robbins stress the intricate relationship between performance during principals' inaugural year and their long-term effectiveness. The first year is a strong predictor of principals' future success, therefore it's imperative they "get it right the first time" (Alvy & Robbins, 1998, p. 15). To this end, the central office has to coordinate the sharing of resources, both human and material, to ensure the development of successful habits early on. Everyone from the personnel department to the business office should care about the newcomer.

Third, the continuous learning and validation of experienced principals is vital. Helping veterans to find more time to focus on instruction, keep abreast of curricular changes, understand evolving state and local mandates, and inspire their staff to reach new heights requires deliberate attention from the central office. Beginning with the school board and filtering through the superintendent, experienced principals should be encouraged to establish meaningful performance goals that extend beyond their comfort zone. These goals must be specific, measurable, and few in number. In addition, offer differentiated, as opposed to one-size-fits-all, professional development to strengthen the knowledge base of veterans. Although there are many parallels between the needs of new and seasoned principals, veterans view challenges and approach problems in different ways. Veterans tend to interpret and translate information differently from new hires because they have more experiences and resources to draw upon. Therefore, training and support should be scaffolded to accommodate these differences.

The work of principals must be valued and recognized at every level of a school district. Socialization activities to help principals combat job isolation and overload are important. Principals need structured opportunities to reflect upon problems and ponder solutions. For instance, in times of massive budget reductions, the superintendent should call principals together to hear their concerns and suggestions before recommending program cuts to the school board. Asking for input gives principals the message that their ideas are important. Individual and group celebrations should also be embedded into the culture so that every principal can share in the victories that come along. Finding and keeping good principals takes a concerted effort on the part of school districts. California's 2001 Superintendent of the Year, James A. Fleming, sums it up best:

> If school boards, superintendents and central office staff fail to recognize the importance of attracting, promoting, and retaining quality principals, who will be left to lead our schools? After all, high stakes testing, increased graduation requirements, and school safety mean little without a principal. (Lovely, 2001, p. 43)

To evaluate an organization's internal effectiveness in administrative development and support, complete the inventory in Figure 1.1. Once areas of strength and need are determined, district leaders can begin to map out a viable recruitment plan to find, select, and hold on to high-quality principals.

FIGURE 1.1

Checklist for Attracting and Retaining High-Quality Administrators

To get a snapshot of how your organization is attracting and retaining high-quality administrators, consider the following behaviors. Once your organization's strengths and weaknesses are identified, focus on a few areas at a time to improve efforts.

Finding High-Quality Candidates	Exceptional	Adequate	Needs Improvement	Does Not Exist
1. The school board and superintendent provide leadership in developing a district recruitment plan.				
2. Principals actively support site-based recruitment efforts.				
3. The Internet is used to accept applications and provide access to information about the district.				
Getting Prospects Ready for the Principalship				
4. The district sponsors administrative preparation programs with local universities.				
5. Entry-level administrative and leadership opportunities are available to prepare prospective candidates from within.				
6. Assistant principals are groomed as instructional leaders and are given a broad range of assignments.				

FIGURE 1.1 *(continued)*

Checklist for Attracting and Retaining High-Quality Administrators

Finding High-Quality Candidates	Exceptional	Adequate	Needs Improvement	Does Not Exist
Supporting a Principal's First Years on the Job				
7. There is a structured orientation to the assigned school for new principals.				
8. Beginning principals are made familiar with the district culture.				
9. Trained coaches and mentors are available to first- and second-year principals.				
Helping Principals Grow				
10. Staff development is designed to support instructional leadership and strengthen the knowledge base of principals.				
11. Training for experienced principals is differentiated and based upon site and individual needs.				
12. Principals are guided in establishing measurable performance goals and are provided dedicated time throughout the year to reflect on these goals.				

FIGURE 1.1 (continued)

Checklist for Attracting and Retaining High-Quality Administrators

Finding High-Quality Candidates	Exceptional	Adequate	Needs Improvement	Does Not Exist
Keeping Good Leaders				
13. Support staff is introduced to help redistribute some of the principal's workload.				
14. Socialization activities, including collegial problem solving, job-alike time, and celebrations, are provided for principals.				
15. The work of a principal is valued and recognized at all levels of the organization.				

Scoring

Give your organization 2 points for every Exceptional response and 1 point for every Adequate response. Award no points for Needs Improvement or Does Not Exist.

Interpretation

0–6 points	Little or no effort exists to attract and grow high-quality leaders inside or outside the district.
7–11 points	Some effort is in place to secure and retain administrative candidates.
12–17 points	The importance of administrative development is on the radar screen. Forward momentum can be noted in one or more areas of principal recruitment.
18–23 points	Substantial progress has been made in finding, developing, and sustaining strong leaders in your district.
24–30 points	Congratulations! Your district is doing a stellar job. The organization serves as a model for others in attracting, inspiring, and holding onto good principals.

Adapted from O'Laughlin, 2001.

2

Finding High-Quality Candidates

If you want one year of prosperity, grow grain. If you want ten years of prosperity, grow trees. If you want one hundred years of prosperity, grow people.

—Chinese Proverb

Take a moment and think back to when you first aspired to become an educator. It's likely that a supervisor, peer, or someone you held in high esteem told you that you'd make a great teacher or administrator. Or maybe you were simply jogging one weekend and in an endorphin-induced euphoria, you heard an inner voice say, "Go forth and broaden your sphere of influence." No matter what form your initial calling took, it is important to realize that educational leaders have the responsibility to mentor the leadership potential in others. One of the greatest gifts we can give back to our profession is to encourage those with promise to become school leaders. Securing effective candidates to take over when we're gone will guarantee a successful future for students, schools, the nation, and the world.

The search for budding leaders needs to be a public affair. Long gone are the days when a school district could sit passively and assume that simply advertising a position would produce desirable candidates. Instead, practitioners from the bottom of the organization to the top must become scouts. Site-based efforts and other internal recruitment strategies should be encouraged and shared.

Current principals are a district's best resource. They have a knack for spotting good talent when they see it and possess firsthand knowledge of what it takes to get the job done.

Once the superintendent and board have made clear that administrative recruitment is a priority, installing a structured career ladder is easy. This effort not only means establishing a grow-your-own program, it also requires districts to promote internal candidates as openings occur. If an administrative development model is established, yet four out of five principalships are filled with outsiders, the internal recruitment scaffold will collapse. Although employing the best available candidate should preclude any guarantee of a promotion, inside applicants will likely be at an advantage if they are identified and mentored by your best people. The actions of the board and superintendent speak volumes about the success or failure of your district's search for prospective leaders—the burden is on them to initiate and sustain an internal recruitment program.

After a district has publicly committed to administrator development, it's important that its scouts know what to look for. Although many aspects of school leadership can be learned, some things may be difficult to teach an adult. Research shows that most principals who lose their jobs do so because of poor interpersonal skills (Davis, 1998). Organizational tasks, unlike people, don't change their mood, need encouragement, or loudly and repeatedly disagree. Working with people requires finesse. An administrator or teacher leader who is perceived to put the organization above people will struggle with human relations because perceptions are reality when it comes to building relationships with others. No matter what a principal says, it's what the staff hears, sees, and feels that counts most in achieving effective school leadership.

It's All About Relationships

Karen Dyer, manager at the Center for Creative Leadership in Greensboro, North Carolina, writes,

> Leaders who are arrogant, dictatorial in their approach, emotionally volatile, and who adopt a bullying style under stress often leave a trail of bruised people. By resisting input from others, ordering people around and making staff feel stupid and unintelligent, leaders set themselves and their organization up for failure. (Dyer, 2001, p. 29)

To foster sound relationships within a school community, the Center for Creative Leadership outlines key competencies that principals-to-be should exhibit:

Ability to Lead: Shows skill in effectively delegating. Provides opportunities and challenges to others. Acts with fairness and brings other talented people into the mix.

Interpersonal Savvy: Possesses skill in building and mending relationships. Shows compassion and sensitivity and is able to put others at ease. Understands and respects cultural, religious, racial, and gender differences.

Work Team Orientation: Effectively listens and communicates by involving others. Strives to build consensus and influence others in the decision-making process.

Conflict Resolution: Employs good timing and common sense in getting objectives accomplished without creating unnecessary adversarial relationships. Recognizes that every decision has opposing interests and constituencies.

Managing Change in Others: Uses effective strategies to facilitate organizational change. Considers the concerns of others and involves key players in the design and implementation of change. Adjusts personal management style to changing situations.

Effectively Confronting Problem Employees: Behaves decisively and skillfully. Handles problem employees with fairness, including those who are loyal but incompetent or ineffective (Dyer, 2001, p. 29).

Dyer points out that relational leadership is not about being "touchy-feely" or sitting around singing "Kumbaya." Rather it's about being in tune with the moods and sentiments of others. Since leadership is situational and varies with individuals and events, it's important that leaders sense what approach to use and when to use it. Highly refined interpersonal skills are necessary to be an effective principal.

To assess your ability to connect with others or to examine the ability of a prospective candidate, use the checklist in Figure 2.1. This checklist can assist in measuring interpersonal know-how and an individual's potential as a developing leader.

In promoting a culture of distributed leadership, the National Staff Development Council reports, "Teachers appear substantially more willing to participate in all areas of decision making if they perceive their relationship with their principal as more open, collaborative, facilitative, and supportive" (Sparks & Hirsh, 2000, p. 8). The key to effective leadership, then, is to accomplish individual and shared goals without damaging relationships and to leave people eager to work with you again. This feat is not always easy to attain, but is always rewarding.

Grow-Your-Own Programs

Although there are many formal programs that encourage paraprofessionals and other classified staff to become teachers, many organizations fall short when it comes to creating similar models for administrative development. Qualified people are available, but too often districts aren't quite sure how to get them on

FIGURE 2.1
Checklist of Relational Leadership Qualities

Check each description that matches the behavior of the person you are considering for a leadership position.

   Candidates with fewer than two qualities in each competency area may not have what it takes to become a relational leader.

Ability to Lead
_____ Helps set instructional goals for the school
_____ Assists a group in staying on course
_____ Brings out the talent in others
_____ Knows when and how to delegate

Interpersonnel Savvy
_____ Knows how to build and mend relationships
_____ Shows respect for cultural, racial, religious, and gender diversity
_____ Puts others at ease through compassion and sensitivity
_____ Puts people first over the organization

Work Team Orientation
_____ Involves others in the decision-making process
_____ Gets commitment from others to do what they say
_____ Knows when and how to use consensus
_____ Encourages, monitors, and rewards group participation

Conflict Resolution
_____ Recognizes visible problems and works to resolve them quickly
_____ Evaluates and interprets information accurately
_____ Values others' points of view
_____ Preserves relationships in resolving conflicts

Managing Change in Others
_____ Involves key players in the implementation of change
_____ Anticipates the concerns of others and the results of her own actions
_____ Adjusts his management style to changing situations
_____ Facilitates collaboration to bring about organizational change

Effectively Confronting Problem Employees
_____ Is not afraid to confront difficult employees, especially when their behavior interferes with the learning and achievement of students
_____ Exercises fairness when handling employee problems
_____ Questions and corrects others in a professional manner
_____ Provides performance feedback and clear expectations based upon evidence and data

Adapted from Dyer, 2001

board. Once a district's scouts have identified potential trainees with the relational know-how to survive the principalship, it's imperative to properly court and groom these candidates.

To select and nurture developing administrators, entry-level positions are simple to design. Caution should be exercised so that organizations do not limit their scope to superstars. If so, expectations will be dashed and few candidates will ever make it past the bottom rung of the career ladder. Instead, entry-level positions must allow promising teacher leaders to get their feet wet—to learn how to do the job—through scaffolded tasks and enculturation.

Although many garden-variety internal recruitment programs are sprouting up around the nation, the Capistrano Unified School District's (CUSD) teaching assistant principal (TAP) model is a standout. Located in Orange County, California, Capistrano is one of the fastest-growing school districts in the state. Between 1993 and 2003, the district built 25 schools. Twenty-nine new principals have been hired since 1998. With this kind of rapid expansion, a significant hurdle for Capistrano is to identify strong administrative candidates ready to move quickly into the principalship. To meet this need, the TAP program has been successfully developed and refined.

Teaching Assistant Principals

The TAP model allows promising leaders the chance to explore the world of administration through scaffolded activities. These activities center around the talents and strengths of each candidate. Principals recruit strong teacher leaders who have the desire to extend themselves beyond their current level of expertise. They invite recruits to try out the role on a year-to-year basis, and closely monitor their progress. Assigned as full-time classroom instructors, TAPs undertake a plethora of additional responsibilities that include curriculum development, committee leadership, coordination of intervention programs, parent and community group liaison, maintaining schedules, textbook inventory and distribution, budget oversight, student discipline, and supervision of personnel. On-site training provides candidates with foundational knowledge of operations so that they can begin to orient themselves toward a bigger view of what it takes to manage and lead a school.

Capistrano's TAP scaffold has a two-tiered structure. Level I TAPs are either considering a career in administration or recently have enrolled in a university program. They remain part of the teachers' bargaining unit and receive an annual stipend of $1,000. A Level II TAP must possess a master's degree and preliminary administrative credentials. They learn to evaluate teaching staff and serve as members of the district's management team. A TAP II is paid a $2,000 annual stipend in addition to their teaching salary. Level II TAPs are eligible to apply for assistant principal openings. Throughout the experience, principals and central office staff give TAPs regular feedback on their progress. The varied opportunities help expand their leadership capacity and provide an excellent springboard for an assistant principal assignment.

At the elementary level, each site is allocated either two Level I elementary TAPs (ETAPs) or one Level II ETAP. For middle and high schools, one secondary TAP (STAP) is selected. Because of flexibility with the master schedule, STAPs are sometimes provided an additional release period during the day for their added duties.

Established in 1965 when district unification first occurred, the TAP program has a long-standing history of success in Capistrano. Half the district's 50 principals started their careers as TAPs. Despite the fact that the district continually looks for candidates from the outside, it has found that internal applicants are often better prepared to face the demands of higher-level administrative positions. See Figure 2.2 (p. 26–27) for a TAP job description.

Teachers on Special Assignment

Another effective entry-level administrative position is a teacher on special assignment (TOSA). A key difference between this position and a teaching assistant principalship is that TOSAs generally do not have full-time classroom responsibilities. Additionally, TOSAs often oversee a particular program or possess a keen subject area focus. They may teach part time or not at all. At the elementary level, for instance, a TOSA might share a 60/40 contract with another teacher, which frees up two or three days per week for them to perform other duties. Or a substitute is sometimes hired to provide coverage on select days throughout the month or year. Middle and high school TOSAs teach anywhere from one to three periods and devote the remainder of their time to a focus area. If a school uses block scheduling, a TOSA can be released up to three full days each week. In some districts, TOSAs relinquish all teaching assignments to concentrate on a single area of emphasis.

In the TOSA model, the candidate oversees a specific program at the site. Examples might include serving as technology coordinator, department chair, activities director, literacy coach, math and science specialist, intervention coordinator, or curriculum leader. The TOSA gains a substantive amount of expertise in program planning and management, budget oversight, scheduling, problem analysis, and facilitating group process. A TOSA may serve on the principal's leadership team and other governing bodies to ensure schoolwide goals are well integrated and articulated. These hands-on experiences allow a candidate to expand leadership skills and help prepare her for a wider range of responsibilities.

To pay for a TOSA, districts have a number of options. The assignment can be included as one full-time equivalent (FTE) in every school's staffing ratio. Or a district can fund a percentage of the allocation (.5 FTE, for instance) and then give flexibility to the principal in making up the difference either through creative master scheduling or the use of site funds. If district and site funds aren't available at all, outside grants or business endowments can be pursued. Principals should be provided alternatives for using a TOSA allocation in the way that best meets their site needs.

FIGURE 2.2

Job Description for a Teaching Assistant Principal

Capistrano Unified School District
Definition
The Teaching Assistant Principal (TAP) is primarily a classroom teacher but will be assigned additional responsibilities under direct supervision of the school principal. Duties performed will also serve as foundational training for the assistant principalship. Candidates are selected by their site principal and recommended for consideration to the Executive Director, Elementary or Secondary School Operations. The primary purpose of the TAP program is to identify and prepare personnel for a position of educational leadership.

Examples of Duties
 • Serves as classroom teacher in assigned subject area or grade level.
 • Assists the principal in curriculum and program design.
 • Assists in the development and maintenance of good school-community relations.
 • Leads site or district committees.
 • Assists in the evaluation of the instructional program and School Improvement Program.
 • Coordinates before and after school intervention programs.
 • Facilitates Student Study Team (SST) and Individualized Education Plan (IEP) meetings.
 • Oversees textbook distribution and inventory.
 • Assists in the development or management of one or two program budgets.
 • Develops and maintains schedules (includes duty, library, computer lab, music, physical education, and art).
 • Serves as liaison to parent groups or other community organizations.
 • Writes columns for school newspaper, weekly updates in the local newspaper, and Parent-Teacher Association newsletters.
 • Helps plan parent education nights.
 • Assists with student discipline.
 • Supervises student events and activities.
 • Assists principal in the supervision and evaluation of teachers and classified staff (Level II only).
 • Attends all Administrative Curriculum Training (ACT) and other professional development for administrators.
 • Serves as Acting Principal of the school in the absence of the principal and assistant principal.

These responsibilities are descriptive only, and the position is not restricted to the tasks listed. It is recommended that each TAP maintain a record of completed activities and experiences.

Qualifications
Knowledge
Principles, methods, goals, and objectives of public education; sound teaching practices that encompass standards-based instruction and learning, curriculum, and assessment trends; procedures and techniques of effective school leadership; student activity, behavior management, and campus supervision; methods and strategies for managing school programs and budgets; strategies for effectively supervising and evaluating personnel.

FIGURE 2.2 *(continued)*

Job Description for a Teaching Assistant Principal

Abilities
Support, organize, and coordinate the management functions and activities of a school; demonstrate positive instructional leadership skills; analyze problems, issues, and concerns, and formulate appropriate solutions; communicate effectively in oral and written form; understand and carry out oral and written directions with minimal accountability and oversight; establish and maintain positive student, staff, parent, and community relations

Experience
Three years of successful teaching experience. Prior administrative or leadership experience is desirable.

Education and Certification Requirement
Level I: A valid California credential authorizing service as a teacher; Administrative Services credential work may or may not be in progress for this assignment.

Level II: A valid California credential authorizing service as a teacher; the completion of a Master of Arts or higher degree from an accredited college or university in Educational Leadership, Curriculum and Instruction, Pupil Personnel, or a closely related field; the possession of a valid Administrative Services credential or Certificate of Eligibility for the Administrative Services credential authorizing service as a California administrator.

Goals of Effective Performance
The goal of the teaching assistant principal is for candidates to successfully perform a variety of instructional and administrative tasks as assigned by the principal. Effective performance will be measured by the principal on an annual basis. Upon completion of successful training and performance, Level II candidates will be given consideration for assistant principal openings. CUSD's policy of employing the best available candidates from both inside and outside the district precludes any guarantee of administrative placement.

Compensation
TAPs will be paid based upon their step and column placement on the teacher's salary schedule. Additional compensation will consist of the following tiers:

Level I: Candidate remains a member of the teacher's bargaining unit, receives a $1,000 annual stipend, and will not formally evaluate personnel.
Level II: Candidate is a part of the Capistrano Unified Management Association (CUMA), receives a $2,000 annual stipend, and may assist the principal in the evaluation of certificated and classified staff.

Adapted with permission from Capistrano Unified School District

The primary purpose of an entry-level training program is to provide a seamless transition for applicants as they step into a leadership role. By empowering principals to appoint and groom these individuals, districts remove unnecessary barriers that might otherwise keep people from the job. It's imperative that entry-level positions be developed in every district to bring reticent leaders with strong potential to the forefront. Entry-level candidates should be mentored by the principal and given honest feedback about their performances. If the principal or candidates find things just aren't working out, the trainees can gracefully return to their previous assignment without a huge investment or loss of face.

Grow-your-own programs are a win for everyone. They can be designed with minimal fiscal impact and risk and are an ideal way to generate high-quality candidates. It takes just one individual to initiate and implement a district model. Could that one person be you?

Establishing University Partnerships

University partnerships are another effective strategy for locating high-quality candidates. In-house administrative certification programs that link institutions of higher education (IHEs) and local school districts provide an excellent bridge to what has often been described as a disjointed system. Part of the problem is that administrative preparation programs are not evolving fast enough to keep up with the standards and accountability movement in schools. University lecture halls, where theory and research often hold sway over practical knowledge, are no longer the best training grounds for principals. According to Mike M. Milstein, professor emeritus in educational administration at the University of New Mexico, many universities are missing the boat by hoarding control of their programs. Milstein says, "We talk partnership with the school district, but the reality is that we don't like to let go" (Keller, 2000, p. 39).

To better align school district needs with principal preparatory programs, partnerships need to be established between a university and a single district or a consortium of districts. The goal of any partnership is to provide more meaningful learning experiences and flexibility to students. Discount tuition rates can be negotiated between the school district and the IHE. With online learning, satellite campuses, and more reasonable licensure requirements, even the most rural districts now have the capability to establish a university partnership.

Several school districts across the country have forged promising relationships with IHEs. In Capistrano Unified, for example, the district has joined forces with Chapman University in Orange, California, to certify candidates for both administrative credentialing tracks that are required by the state. The program holds classes at the central office, limits class size to 20 participants, and provides experienced instructors from inside and outside the district. The curriculum is tailored to meet university requirements as well as district needs. The Capistrano-Chapman partnership is a symbiotic undertaking. District employees appreciate the academic quality, convenience, and reduced tuition, while the university fulfills its mission of reaching out to a broader constituency.

In Madison, Wisconsin, the school district and the University of Wisconsin–Madison have designed a blended program that relies on retired principals to mentor participants. The program includes a yearlong internship and provides meaningful university coursework. An array of program graduates has been readied to move into leadership assignments.

In Kentucky, the University of Louisville has hooked up with the Jefferson County School District to offer the Identifying and Developing Educational Administrators for Schools (IDEAS) program. After being nominated by their principals, candidates apply to the university for acceptance. Admissible candidates are then formally invited to participate in the IDEAS cohort by the school district. A professor is assigned by the university to teach the coursework, which includes curriculum modules designed by the National Association of Secondary School Principals (NASSP). In addition, participants receive intensive training in leading their schools within the context of Kentucky's standards-based account-ability system. This cooperative endeavor has received accolades throughout the region.

Rural districts face unique challenges in finding aspiring adminis-trators. The difficulty lies in enticing teachers with leadership poten-tial to explore the possibilities of a principalship. The common drawbacks for teachers are a desire to remain in the same school and community, insufficient compensation, and lack of convenience in entering a training program. To overcome these obstacles, a district can support attendance at national institutes such as the Harvard University and Vanderbilt University summer academies. By sending one or two aspiring leaders to a national institute, a rural district can show a prospective administrator a new world of opportunities. Most participants return from these academies with an inspired focus to lead.

To combat an absence of interest in working in rural states, dis-tricts have responded to the recruitment problem through a multipronged approach, which includes collaboration from state agencies, universities, and professional organizations. The Shields Valley School District in Montana serves as a stellar example of how such efforts can work. Shields Valley encompasses two small towns in a single district serving roughly 300 students. The elementary principal is assigned to oversee schools in both communities, which are 10 miles apart. The low-paying position makes it hard to attract a dynamic principal from a large applicant pool. When the superin-tendent recognized the problem several years ago, he worked with the Montana Office of Public Instruction and the two universities in the state, Montana State University and the University of Montana, to establish an administrative development program. This program incorporates an internship with a provisional certification requirement. Part of the certification involves summer coursework and a university contract to provide qualified mentors. In addition, Montana's elementary and secondary professional associations have waived registration fees to their annual conferences for these prospective administrators. Special sessions for candidates and their mentors are also offered at these conferences. Program evaluations have been favorable and principals who have been promoted through this vehicle are highly rated by their superintendents.

Administrators Are Teachers, Too

As universities adapt to the fluctuation in career trends, job markets, and learner profiles, adjunct professors are becoming increasingly more popular in graduate-level studies. According to a recent article in the *New York Times' Education Life,* some 43 percent of the nation's college faculty is part-time. This is great news for the field of education because 21st-century administration is less about theory and more about practical, ethical, and moral applications of leadership. Ohio State professor Joseph Murphy describes the shifting focus of modern-day preparation programs from "educational administration as management to educational administration primarily concerned with teaching and learning" (Murphy, 2001, p. 15). With this changed emphasis, the relationship between universities and local school districts continues to become more and more important.

Those with firsthand knowledge and intuition about what it takes to be a principal should be teaching prospective administrators. We cannot afford to have someone who hasn't stepped foot in a school for 20 years to be training future leaders. Practicing superintendents, principals, central office administrators, and other qualified personnel are encouraged to pursue positions as part-time faculty. Serving as an adjunct professor also puts a district employee in the enviable position of scouting for good talent. There's the added benefit, too, of being back in the classroom and close to the adults who know best about the underpinnings of school-related issues. As part-time professors, we can listen and learn from the site-based experts and become more effective in our own positions of leadership.

Planting seeds to grow a new crop of leaders should be a team effort. And teamwork doesn't tolerate the inconvenience of distance (HeartMath Quotes, 2003). Forming partnerships with universities in conjunction with the development of an internal recruitment career ladder presents a winning combination. As your district searches for high-quality candidates, putting this scaffold in place is a breeze once someone decides to step up to the plate and make it happen.

3
Getting Prospects Ready for the Principalship

The final test of a leader is that he leaves behind him in other men the conviction and will to carry on.

—Walter Lippmann

Everything educators know about good teaching tells us that some of the best learning takes place when authentic experiences are embedded into the curriculum. Learning to drive a car, for example, would be impossible if we only read about it in the driver's education manual. We could fill our heads with all the legal and technical elements of driving, but until we get behind the wheel we don't have the chance to practice what we've been taught. Can you imagine heading over to the department of motor vehicles on your 16th birthday and trying to pass the driving test without this hands-on training?

Many of the country's most important professions require some kind of simulated learning before licensure can occur. Coursework for preparing teachers, doctors, pilots, and police officers includes such simulated learning. When it comes to the principalship, however, our future leaders are expected to conquer the motorway without any behind-the-wheel experience. University programs alone will never be enough to prepare principals for the day-to-day challenges of the job. Why?

In the university you spend extended periods reflecting about a problem and solution; in the principalship, problem resolution is expected yesterday. In a university class, you might read a case study on searching a school locker for drugs and debate with classmates whether the search should be conducted. As a principal, you hear about possible drugs in a locker ten minutes before dismissal; you need to act quickly. (Alvy & Robbins, 1998, p. 9)

To prepare candidates for the principalship, opportunities are needed to replicate the true conditions under which a principal must work. Because principals manage complex organizations with unpredictable demands, they sometimes find it hard to maintain a clear sense of purpose. Kent Peterson, renowned author of several books on school leadership, describes the following central features of a principal's job as the greatest obstacles to overcome:

- Brevity
- Variety
- Fragmentation

The following adapted diary of a middle school principal, first published by the University of California Santa Cruz's New Administrator Program, captures Peterson's thoughts perfectly:

My Life in the Past 25 Days

1. Car fire: cleaned up foam, melted rubber, and soot before students arrived.

2. Called maintenance to repaint, replace melted light fixtures, and repair field where fire truck got stuck.

3. Calmed community hysteria that a terrorist group had tried to bomb the school.

4. Replaced 7 indoor locks that the fire marshall cited when inspecting the fire.

5. Suspended 9 students for fighting.

6. Informed 2 temporary teachers that they would not be rehired next year.

7. Received formal complaint against the custodian (resulted in letter of reprimand).

8. Parent complained that the nurse didn't call her when her child had a tummy ache (even though the parent has no phone).

9. Parent complained about other parents not talking to her. (Call made to the assistant superintendent that I have a "gang" of parents who are against her.)

10. Reassigned a special ed teacher after allegation of discrimination against a student. (Lawsuit pending.)

11. Hired long-term sub for special education class. Called all parents in the class.

12. New special education teacher and aides do not get along. All complain and demand changes.

13. New special education teacher takes two weeks off for back injury. (Unknown if returning.)

14. A parent tells two teachers I'm conspiring to get them fired.

15. Filed two reports with child protective services about suspected abuse.

16. Media clerk has a family emergency and is gone the entire week before the annual book fair. (Set up the book fair with my secretary.)

17. Media clerk gives two-week notice.

18. Staff member finds out she has cancer.

19. Attended eight evening meetings and events.

20. Four 8th-grade girls falsely accused a male teacher of looking at them in a sexual way.

21. Distributed staff survey to receive feedback on my leadership skills.

22. Spent numerous hours looking at blueprints for the school renovation project.

23. Planned and conducted a full-day workshop for faculty on curriculum mapping.

24. Lead reflective conference with math department to analyze our standardized test scores.

25. Continued documenting a 20-year veteran who is having significant performance issues. (adapted from New Teacher Center, 2002b)

Prospective candidates gearing up for the intricacies of school leadership, as seen in this diary, must be cognizant of potential roadblocks and figure out how to get around them. Waiting to practice
this maneuver until teacher leaders are sitting in the principal's
chair is simply too late. Through a deeper examination of the managerial and symbolic challenges of brevity, variety, and fragmentation, districts can design in-house training modules that will prepare
future principals for the calamities that lie ahead. Let's examine
these challenges briefly.

Living with Brevity

A principal's work consists of many tasks short in duration and
rapid in pacing. Most exchanges last from one to two minutes. This
means a principal might face 50 or 60 activities in a single hour. In
fact, 85 percent of a principal's time is spent on tasks lasting less
than nine minutes (Peterson, 1982). These brief encounters require
more energy than longer activities and can exasperate even the most
steel-nerved individual. Problems and their respective solutions
must be analyzed quickly. Additionally, the principal is often the
only link between several detached groups. In this linking capacity,
the principal is continually connecting "component to component,
the school unit to the region, and the school to the wider environment" (Peterson, 1982, p.1).

To learn to live with the aspects of brevity, prospective principals
must develop the capacity to handle a world full of brief engage-
ments. The ability to think on their feet is a must. During training,
candidates should learn to assess situations swiftly and accurately.
Understanding the pace and accepting that tasks need to be completed in bits and pieces allows candidates to feel competent and

confident. Tackling the brevity of the principalship is far less stress-ful if expectations to manage conditions, rather than resist them, are clear from the start. Like mastering a manual transmission, train-ees must be able to "shift from first to second and back without grinding gears" (Peterson, 2001, p. 20).

The Vexation of Variety

The daily tasks and assignments of the principalship vary greatly. Duties require diverse skills, technical capability, and various levels of cognitive functioning. One minute a principal may be trying to balance the school's budget; the next minute a principal may be called upon to console a frantic teacher who just learned her hus-band has fallen ill. Most interactions involve human contact, which is more time-intensive and emotionally taxing than facing inani-mate problems. Additionally, principals have to connect with sev-eral age groups, ranging from young children to older adults. With the wide range in age comes a greater variety of responses. A 20-something teacher has a different point of reference than a 54-year-old classroom veteran. A first-time mom may become hys-terical when she receives a discipline call from the principal, while a grandfather who has custody of his teenage grandson takes it all in stride. Trying to anticipate and address the disparate needs of such a broad constituency can leave principals feeling like hamsters on a wheel. Relentlessly, they labor to juggle the completion of tasks against the preservation of relationships.

To tackle the variety of relationships, the principalship calls for technical and interpersonal savvy. Although organizational know-how is important, beginners need to pay close attention to their human resources. Principals need to know how to frame con-versations in a way that acknowledges the unique expectations of diverse interest groups. By exercising good judgment and taking the time to listen, principals-in-the-making will garner the trust and respect necessary to shape a positive and collaborative culture. Leadership lessons in interpersonal intelligence will be explored further in Chapter 4.

Frustrating Fragmentation

A principal's job is fraught with fragmentation. New projects, problems, and crises regularly interrupt the cycle of ongoing activities. A principal must simultaneously provide information, cope with workflow issues, and make short-term and long-term decisions. The higher the volume of concurrent obstacles, the more fragmented a principal's life can become. On top of all this, other people actually initiate a large proportion of a principal's tasks. Bombarded with requests from every corner of the district, above and below on the organizational chart, principals are forever caught in the middle.

To be competent, principals-in-training must function under fragmented circumstances. They should come to the role with strong coping skills and have a vivid understanding of the complex nature of the job. With so many competing factions vying for the principal's attention, a trainee has to take the lead in setting priorities for herself and others. Time management, sound organizational skills, and effective delegation are vital to survival. The ability to quickly prioritize important issues, define time constraints, and maintain mental fortitude will help prospective leaders remain focused. To control the fragmentation without losing equilibrium, they must learn to compartmentalize each request and assignment. This means homing in on one situation before another encroaches upon their effectiveness (McCormack, 2000). For example, if a candidate finishes a hostile meeting with a parent and then rushes off to deliver a perfect attendance award to a student, he might appear distracted or short with the youngster. Delaying the classroom visit until emotions are in check is a way to separate the events.

Escaping the Grips of Dependency

What does all this mean for aspiring principals? To prepare for the principalship, assignments that combine brevity, variety, and fragmentation are essential. Real-world experiences should be integrated into the training regimen and teach future school leaders how to do the following:

- Work quickly, but know when to take time to solve a problem.
- Finish tasks in tiny bits and pieces throughout the day.
- Organize volumes of information, events, incidents, and demands all at the same time.
- Apply key skills that lead to organizational effectiveness such as delegation, forecasting, shared decision making, problem analysis, and time management.
- Define what information is important in addressing critical issues.
- Reflect on "How is what I'm doing helping move our school toward its goal?"
- Get to know the school's constituency and community needs.
- Enjoy the ride through networking, storytelling, and relationship building. (Peterson, 2001, p. 20)

A principal cannot act as an instructional leader if these basic features of the job are overlooked. When the inherent complexities of the job go unmanaged, the teaching and learning agenda is pushed aside while other less important events consume the principal's day. When principals become overloaded, an environment of dependency permeates the school (Fullan, 1998). The context for dependency occurs as principals find themselves on the receiving end of changes initiated by everyone else. Nonstop changes prolong the brief, fragmented, and varied working conditions that keep principals off balance and on edge. Consequently, principals become insecure about making their own decisions, causing them to either ask for permission to do things or to wait for answers from outside the school. This ineffective use of power and authority on the part of the principal reinforces similar behavior among teachers. Dependency can paralyze a school.

To avoid the grips of dependency, scaffolded experiences that expose future leaders to the brevity, variety, and fragmentation of the role should be provided before a candidate steps into the principal's office. Rather than searching for the silver bullet to make the job easier, trainees must look for answers within themselves.

Getting the Experience to Your Candidates

Traditional university coursework characterizes most administrative preparation programs across the United States; still, some school districts have taken bold steps to find a better way to equip teacher leaders for the principalship. Apprentice and intern programs allow prospects to get into the trenches and discover firsthand what it means to be a learning leader. Apprentice and intern programs for aspiring principals are an excellent means of getting that experience to your candidates.

In school administration, apprenticeships and internships are generally regarded as interchangeable. However, if we turn to *Webster's New World Dictionary*, we see a difference in how these terms are defined. An *intern* is described as "an advanced student or recent graduate undergoing supervised practical training." An *apprentice* is identified as "one bound by a legal document to work for another for a specific amount of time in return for instruction in the trade, art or business." In the various support systems being implemented by school districts, an internship appears to be a more formalized assignment lasting anywhere from one to two years. A few principal interns fly solo in the role and are paired with an off-site mentor. But most interns work beside a master principal. Principal internships are often tied to university certification programs.

Apprenticeships, on the other hand, are shorter in duration, lasting anywhere from 6 to 18 weeks, and generally do not involve corresponding university coursework. Program development and support for the apprentice comes solely from site or district personnel. Apprentices spend a greater amount of time "shadowing" the master principal and learn through observation, inquiry, reflection, and modeling.

Apprenticeships for Aspiring Leaders

In the Boston Public Schools (BPS), the Principal Prep program is a stellar example of how a successful apprenticeship can be structured. The program, which began in 1998, solicits in-house participants from among assistant principals, central office administrators, teachers nearing completion of a university credentialing program, licensed employees who have chosen not to activate their administrative credential, and doctoral students. After an initial paper screening, the field of nearly 80 applicants is narrowed to between 25 and 40 semifinalists. These semifinalists are led through a series of demonstration projects conducted on a Saturday. The demonstration projects call upon applicants to

- Review and critique a videotaped classroom lesson and then illustrate how they would guide the teacher in a reflective postobservation conference.
- Compose a letter to faculty or families about a timely district issue to assess the candidate's on-demand writing ability.
- Complete an in-basket exercise to measure organizational and prioritization skills.
- Participate in a decision-making activity with other applicants to reveal how they behave in groups, what roles they assume, and their ability to function as a collaborative team member. (Curtis, 2002)

Following this daylong assessment, about a dozen finalists are scheduled for personal interviews with a screening team. Each successful candidate is then invited to work as an apprentice in one of Boston's 135 public schools.

The BPS principal apprenticeships run concurrently for eight weeks from early February to mid-April. Before candidates ever step into the role, they attend a six-day induction session. Once the actual assignment begins, weekly seminars and specific field projects are embedded into the training to offer a balanced and comprehensive experience. By the end of the eight weeks, apprentices return to their previous assignment with a renewed sense of confidence and knowledge about what it takes to be a principal. They are also ready and able to apply for any of the dozen annual principal openings in the Boston Public Schools. Between 60 and 75 percent of those who complete the endeavor get hired in the district, which speaks volumes about the success of Boston's Principal Prep program.

Although the BPS apprentice model is an excellent means of preparing candidates for the principalship, it is not without its drawbacks. According to Rachel Curtis, Boston's director of school development (personal communication, August 2002), the primary obstacle is finding coverage for apprentices during the eight weeks they are gone from their regular assignment. This means that the principal or supervisor at the site where the candidate is assigned has to be willing to support the endeavor. The goal is to ensure that the program, which can become quite labor intensive, does not shift any burden from one principal to another. Additionally, master principals need to be carefully selected. Although many veterans may be eager for an extra pair of hands on their campuses, serving as a master principal requires a significant commitment. Not all experienced principals are cut out to be mentors. Therefore, a good match between apprentice and master principal is crucial. To compensate the Boston principals for their efforts, a $500 to $1,000 stipend is offered. It may seem like a nominal amount, yet it sends a powerful message to the veterans that they are appreciated for giving back to their profession.

Another noteworthy apprentice model can be found in the Chicago Public Schools' Leadership, Academy & Urban Network for Chicago program (LAUNCH). LAUNCH incorporates a semester-long paid fellowship with a five-week summer leadership academy at Northwestern University. By collaborating with Northwestern faculty and the Chicago Principals and Administrators Association (CPAA), LAUNCH staff ensures the preparation of principals is balanced, rigorous, and meaningful.

The LAUNCH program, which is organized around the district's seven leadership standards (see Figure 3.1), is intended to accelerate, intensify, and deepen the knowledge, skills, and experiences individuals have prior to selection as a principal. A unique feature of the apprenticeship is that three of the 18 weeks are served at a different school level. This means that elementary fellows spend a portion of their time on a middle or high school campus while the secondary fellows go to an elementary site. The switch not only broadens the awareness candidates have for what takes place at other levels, it also changes some apprentices' minds about where they want to work.

FIGURE 3.1
Chicago Standards for Developing Leaders

Standard 1: School Leadership
Standard 2: Parent Involvement and Community Partnerships
Standard 3: Creating Student-Centered Learning Climates
Standard 4: Professional Development and Human Resource Management
Standard 5: Instructional Leadership: Improving Teaching and Learning
Standard 6: School Management and Daily Operations
Standard 7: Interpersonnel Effectiveness

From the Chicago Principals and Administrators Association (CPAA, 2002)

Up to 30 of Chicago's best and brightest are chosen each year to serve as fellows. Candidates are selected through an extensive screening process that closely parallels the Boston model. A primary difference, however, is that LAUNCH holds a "matching day" to pair mentors and candidates. Principals and fellows gather in a large auditorium and meet one another through 10-minute interviews. By the end of the day, participants submit a list of five people with whom they'd like to work. LAUNCH staff then sort through the lists to find the right match based upon principal-fellow recommendations, interests, and expectations.

To be considered for an apprenticeship, applicants must be employed in the district and already hold a Type 75 Illinois certificate. The Chicago School Board allocates $1.2 million annually to support the program, which covers the $77,000 salary for each fellow. This sends a cogent message to current and future leaders about the importance the board places on the development of strong principals. The LAUNCH credo—"Be relentless about improving learning"—is exemplified through actions as Chicago's budding leaders are readied for the principalship (CPAA, 2002).

Intern Models That Work

Another pathway to the principalship is through a well-designed intern program. A smattering of school districts throughout the country allows current employees to serve as interns while they earn credit toward principal licensure. The Madison Metropolitan School District, for example, offers two paid internships each year. To be considered, candidates must either hold a current administrative license or be able to meet the requirements of Wisconsin's Department of Public Instruction within 12 months of starting the internship.

Madison's authentic leadership experience permits the two selected candidates to spend a full year working closely with a cooperating principal. Each intern learns the skills and art of being a principal through deliberate experiences that blend operational management with ongoing development as an instructional leader. Specific training includes using student achievement data to make decisions and inform curriculum and staff development, budget planning, facilities and scheduling, student discipline, problem solving and conflict resolution, as well as building a positive school culture and community relationships. Interns also participate in the district's monthly beginning-principals' colloquium and attend University of Wisconsin intern meetings during the first semester.

Upon appropriate certification and successful completion of the internship, candidates are invited to apply for principal vacancies in the Madison Metropolitan School District. If recommended, the intern must agree to accept employment as a principal or continue to work in the district for at least two years beyond the internship. The goal in Madison is to develop and nurture the leadership potential of talented district staff and to provide a more diverse applicant pool for principal positions. Madison's belief that internships are "an opportunity for tomorrow's principals to learn from today's educational leaders" symbolizes the district's commitment to helping candidates get ready for the principalship (Madison Metropolitan School District, 2002).

In the greater Charlotte area, the University of North Carolina (UNC) has established the two-year Principal Fellows program that is supported by $20,000 scholarship loans from the state. After university students finish their first year of classroom study, they are eligible to be placed as interns in one of 23 participating school districts. The remaining course credits, which include units for fieldwork, are taken concurrently with the yearlong intern assignment. UNC faculty works with school district personnel to arrange for students to be compensated during their internship. Success stories abound, as 25 percent of the 442 graduates have become principals. Here's how one exuberant intern described her experience at Kannapolis Middle School in Kannapolis, North Carolina:

In June 1997 I began a journey that would become the most exciting and rewarding experience of my life. Throughout my internship year, I was challenged to put into practice all that I had learned in my master's program. I cannot imagine what it would have been like venturing into the position of assistant principal or principal without this experience. However, I realize that there are many individuals across the nation participating in school administration programs that do not require internships. To me, this is the greatest injustice that we do to aspiring leaders of our schools. (Gray, 2001, p. 663)

Tips for a Successful Training Module

As a district makes plans to implement an apprentice or intern training module in their organization, six important elements should be incorporated into the program structure (Gray, 2001). These elements will help guarantee that the participant and principal find the undertaking mutually beneficial and rewarding:

1. Assimilate the mentor and candidate into their roles: Let them develop a relationship by bringing the two together at least a month before the assignment begins. Choose mentors skilled at teaching adults and train them in effective coaching strategies.

2. Make the assignment full time: To provide a high-quality experience, the interns or apprentices should be fully released from their existing assignment. This allows the candidates to concentrate entirely on their training. If funds are available, yearlong assignments are the ideal. But even an eight-week experience can be extremely effective.

3. Create a shared purpose: To prevent a haphazard venture, the leadership standards adopted by your district or state can be used to ground the experience. If goals are identified and mutually agreed upon at the beginning of the assignment, both parties will benefit. Key achievements of the internship should be tied to the standards and goals. For example, one

goal is for the intern to become more skilled at helping teachers use multiple assessments to evaluate instruction and learning. The intern and master principal can create a grade level or departmental meeting agenda designed to bring small groups of teachers together to look at data. The intern serves as the sage on the stage, while the principal acts as a guide on the side. Later, as the intern and master principal debrief about the meeting, follow-up activities are planned based upon the staff's dialogue and discoveries during the exercise.

4. Increase responsibilities gradually: In the beginning, the intern or apprentice must spend time shadowing the principal. As both become more comfortable, responsibilities can be added incrementally to the intern's role. Responsibilities should extend beyond basic managerial duties and probe the depths of instructional leadership. At first the intern might simply watch the principal conduct a few lesson observations and postobservation conferences with teachers. The intern should pay careful attention to the inquiry-based questions asked by the master principal. When ready, the intern can then conduct a formal lesson observation and have the principal review her written summary before going over it with the teacher. At the conclusion of the postobservation conference, the principal and intern should reflect on what impact the meeting had on the teacher.

5. Set aside time for daily reflection and evaluation: Time has to be devoted to reflect and debrief about daily events and issues. As the participant's "critical friend," the master principal needs to provide constructive feedback and guidance. Candidates should feel comfortable asking questions as they strive for ways to improve.

6. Rely on the university supervisor or district program coordinator if problems arise: A venue for providing additional support or advice to the master principal and participant should

be available. Partnering with a university exposes candidates to ideas from outside the district. A third party can also make certain the shared vision and program goals are followed. Any successful intern or apprentice program is built around time, commitment, and resources (Gray, 2001, pp. 663–665).

Although this kind of principal preparation is not without costs, it provides one of the best on-the-job training opportunities on the market. You can read and study all the latest books about becoming an effective principal, but nothing can beat experience. By hand-picking teacher leaders to serve as interns or apprentices, we can equip them with the necessary training and practice to ease into the role of principal. With enhanced certainty about what it takes to get the job done, these trainees are ready and eager to sit in the principal's chair.

Virtual Principal

Computer-based simulation programs, formerly only in the hands of military installations and flight schools, are the latest high-tech craze in the private sector. *U.S. News and World Report* recently declared that within the next four years, 70 percent of all corporate e-learning will include some kind of virtual reality training (Boser, 2002).

SimuLearn, a Connecticut-based company, has created a program called Virtual Leader that immerses managers in a series of real-life business scenarios via the Internet or a CD. Programs range from handling daily operational tasks to de-escalating tension between hostile employees and clients. Other gaming software on the market even has an "electronic mentor" who guides users through choppy waters. "People learn by practicing; by making mistakes," says Clark Aldrich, vice president of SimuLearn (Boser, p. 60). Users can repeat sessions and try alternate approaches to see how the results differ when other solutions are explored.

Could the Virtual Principal be in our future? There's no reason why not. Although the educational content might vary from business world content, the issues faced by school leaders parallel the issues plaguing many senior level managers. It seems prudent, then, for universities and educational organizations to explore the use of e-learning as a means of expanding existing curriculum. Although there's no substitute for real-life experience, interactive computer simulation is a way to augment traditional coursework with hands-on training.

Grooming Your Assistant Principals

Overwhelming evidence indicates that public school leadership today is unconventional and complicated (ERS, 2000). To ready a candidate for the principalship, streamlined activities must be available at every level of preparation. These activities should extend beyond the basic managerial functions of administration and reach into the heart and soul of instructional leadership—the purpose of which is to enhance student and adult learning. Let's take a closer look at how assistant principals are currently groomed and examine the effectiveness of existing support systems. An excellent assistant principal doesn't always make the best principal. Without depth and complexity in his experience, an assistant principal may be able to manage a school but will struggle to lead it.

Traditionally, the role of the assistant principal has been designed for an individual to serve as a "subadministrator" rather than a "coadministrator." Assistant principals perform what are typically operational responsibilities at the school level. Duties might include handling student discipline, master scheduling, supervising events, resolving parent complaints, and overseeing facility needs. Assistant principals often stay behind to hold down the fort while principals are away at district meetings and inservice training. It is then left to the principals to bring the assistant principals up to speed on whatever is introduced by the central office. Messages are sometimes diluted or simply forgotten as principals hurriedly return to their busy schedules, leaving the assistant principals out of the loop regarding current concerns and issues.

If assistant principal assignments are to serve as a pathway to the principalship, the expectations and experiences of the position must be expanded. Assistant principals need ample opportunities to develop individual capacity and gain exposure to key leadership components. Every curriculum, instruction, evaluation, and assessment topic principals learn about should also be available to assistant principals. When a site administrative team sits down to discuss how it will introduce a new process or innovation to the staff, the results can be powerful when everyone has the same point of reference and information. If the principal is the sole keeper of the knowledge, a shared commitment cannot be sustained. As each school strives to become a professional learning community, the principal has to ensure that coadministrators function as a collaborative and cohesive unit. To do so requires a conscious effort at both the site and the district level.

One way to strengthen the skills of an entire administrative team is to establish yearly performance goals for each member. Performance goals, which rarely are written by assistant principals, should be based upon individual needs, anticipated school outcomes, and the principal's expectations. The creation of a professional portfolio that includes artifacts, a reflection journal, notes from teachers and parents, and other evidence can be used to measure progress. A mid-year conference with the principal will verify whether coadministrators are on course. In the spring, the principal should complete a formal evaluation to record commendations, noted growth, and suggestions for continued improvement. Passing the assistant principal in the hallway and saying, "You're doing a great job!" is not enough. Assistant principals, like teachers, need specific feedback and deliberate strategies to improve. Training and support from the central office and outside educational agencies must be ongoing. These combined efforts will validate the hard work of assistant principals and let them know that what they do is important.

When Sherine Smith was principal at Capistrano Valley High School (CVHS) in Mission Viejo, California, she used the strategy of empowerment to foster personal leadership development in her assistant principals. The A-Team, consisting of the principal, four assistant principals, a teaching assistant principal, and the activities director, clearly understood and shared the school's mission and vision. Smith assigned each team member specific managerial duties to divide the workload. However, student learning, the examination of instructional practice, curriculum alignment, and data-driven decision making were the responsibility of the collective group. Smith was keenly aware that to have an effective A-Team, roles needed to reflect broad involvement and collaboration. In this way, the talents of every team member were tapped. This type of infrastructure supports self-renewal, collective inquiry, and a shared commitment toward improvement (Lambert, 1998).

Through ongoing monitoring and evaluation of school goals, the coadministrators at CVHS learned to skillfully participate in the leadership process described in Linda Lambert's *Building Leadership Capacity in Schools* (1998). Following Smith's promotion to the central office, assistant principal Tom Ressler was a natural successor. As a result, a unified message about what is truly important continues to flow from every artery of the school. The A-team meets regularly with department chairs and teacher leaders to engage in conversations that call for action rather than passivity. Unobstructed communication loops generate two-way feedback at all levels of the organization. The well-apportioned leadership at CVHS has "direction and momentum, [as] it negotiates through passages" (Lambert, 1998, p. 8).

To empower her assistant principals and ensure the continuous development of a strong A-Team, Smith used Lambert's capacity-building guidelines as her roadmap:

- Leadership and leader are not the same; leadership isn't based upon specific traits and qualities.
- Leadership is about learning that leads to collective change.
- Everyone in the organization has the potential and the right to work as a leader.
- Leading is a shared endeavor.
- Leadership requires the redistribution of power and authority. (Lambert, 1998, p. 8–9)

Smith's ability to look beyond the obvious and ferret out the potential in each individual served to cultivate multiple groups to get the work done. Space and time are still set aside for the A-team to grapple with tough issues. Roles and responsibilities are designed to give assistant principals the chance to put their leadership skills into practice. Several avenues to demonstrate proficiency are available. A comprehensive list of suggested activities for developing leaders designed by Capistrano Unified School District's Education Division (CUSD, 2000) provides the impetus to ensure that every coadministrator in the district experiences the various dimensions of the job (see Appendix A). During her eight years as a middle and high school principal, Smith epitomized how the principalship is used to bring along new leaders—and she did it all with incredible skill, humility, and ease.

No single-best system exists to prepare prospective principals for the job. Candidates can come from all segments of the educational community and might have varying styles of leadership. As your district works to ready prospects for the principalship, remember that candidates will benefit most from an abundance of opportunities and experiences. The goal is to expose future leaders to the routine challenges and chaotic events of the day while modeling how to maintain an ironclad grip on the learning focus. Getting ready for the principalship is substantially less overwhelming when people are able to work with things as they are, not as they hoped they were, or think they ought to be.

4

Supporting a Principal's First Years on the Job

At times it's like I'm maneuvering in a minefield. Things blow up and I crawl out of the hole.

—First-year principal, New Administrator Program

The Story of the Little Red Hen

One balmy September afternoon, the Little Red Hen sat down to read her e-mail messages. She was just completing her first month as the new principal of the Hen House, and it was already 6 p.m. Where had the day gone? After sorting through all her memos and messages, she found herself pecking out a very long "To Do" list.

The next morning the Little Red Hen approached her three teacher friends and inquired: "Who will help me write our school plan?"

"Not I!" squealed Mrs. Piggy. "I have two little piglets at home."

"Not I!" quacked Mr. Mallard. "I have a doctor's appointment today."

"Not I!" meowed Miss Catty. "I'm not a very good writer."

"Then I will write the plan all by myself," replied the Little Red Hen. After all, the plan was due in two weeks. What would the Central Farm say if the Little Red Hen turned hers in late?

That winter the Hen House goals sprouted and grew until they turned into great big action steps. So the Little Red Hen bravely returned to her teacher friends and beseeched, "Who will help me organize our after-school reading intervention program?"

"Not I!" meowed Miss Catty. "My kindergarten kittens don't need interventions."

"Not I!" quacked Mr. Mallard. "I already teach reading during the school day."

"Not I!" squealed Mrs. Piggy. "I go to the gym after school to reduce my stress."

"Then I will organize the reading intervention program all by myself," said the Little Red Hen. And she found tutors, created the curriculum, and made the schedule with nary a lick of assistance!

In the spring, the Little Red Hen went back to her teacher friends and stoically asked, "Who will help me organize our Parent Education Night?"

"Not I!" quacked Mr. Mallard. "I don't do well with parents."

"Not I!" meowed Miss Catty. "I only do things at night if I'm paid."

"Not I!" squealed Mrs. Piggy. "Parent Education won't do a lick of good with the kind of students in our pen."

"Then I will get the Do Bees to plan our Parent Education Night," squawked the Little Red Hen. After all, what would the community think if she were the only principal in town who didn't offer parent training? So the Do Bees—who always do everything—planned the whole thing themselves!

On the last day of school Mr. Mallard, Miss Catty, and Mrs. Piggy hugged good-bye before dashing off for their summer vacations. Back in her office, the Little Red Hen was asleep atop her computer. It was no surprise that she was exhausted after such a productive inaugural year. As for the Do Bees, they were sprawled around the Hen House floor. Some were dazed and confused while others were trying to recover from broken wings and lost stingers. A few Do Bees had gathered the strength to fly south to a more peaceful and moderate climate. They told the Little Red Hen and the others around the Hen House to buzz off!

The story of the Little Red Hen strikes a chord in many of us. Perhaps we've succumbed to the role ourselves, or maybe we've watched with empathy as a principal acquaintance has struggled to do all and be all. Etched in our minds is the now familiar list of reasons why it's difficult to attract and retain people in the principalship. Long hours, an excessive workload, and insurmountable expectations from several opposing factions can lead to unmanageable stress. These stressors plague nearly every principal, but beginners face the added challenges brought on by inexperience. Without a doubt, the first year of the principalship is the most challenging. One Colorado study, for example, found that stress for first-timers falls into three major categories: (1) absorbing volumes of information; (2) working for change despite significant resistance; and (3) proving oneself to others (Strong, Barret, & Bloom, 2002). Because beginning principals have yet to establish relationships and gain credibility with staff, parents, the central office, and the community, they regularly suffer from a sense of helplessness, insecurity, and fear of failure. Like our Little Red Hen, the inability of novice principals to effectively delegate and share leadership responsibilities makes them especially vulnerable.

Transitioning into the Principalship

Being a school principal has been likened to being the mayor of a small town (Yerkes & Guaglianone, 1998). Although the celebrity status is a great ego boost, it comes at a price. As new principals enter the position, they adapt to the role at different rates of speed. The transition period for a beginner, also referred to as the "socialization process," is characterized by three distinct stages: (1) the anticipatory stage, (2) the encounter stage, and (3) the insider stage (Alvy & Robbins, 1998, p. 4).

The anticipatory stage commences as soon as the candidate accepts the job and starts to sever ties with current colleagues. As old loyalties are broken, new alliances are formed. When the principal looks forward to the position, yet ardently remembers previous relationships and responsibilities, it's considered "healthy leave taking." On the other hand, when new principals struggle to let go of the past or maintain a selective memory about how wonderful things were in their former assignments, they may remain stuck in this stage. The success of beginning principals largely depends upon how adeptly they transition into their role and environment.

Once newcomers are handed the keys to the school, they begin to deal with the issues, routines, and relationships of uncharted territory. This second transitional phase is called the encounter stage. For many, this stage is fraught with loneliness, logistical challenges, time constraints, and complex relationships. The induction period for first-timers is relatively short. If the newcomer cannot quickly understand and handle these encounters with so many different constituents, it becomes increasingly difficult to recover in subsequent years. Patterns and habits are hard to change. Success during the encounter stage is gauged by what the principal pays attention to, how the principal reacts to crisis, the principal's words and deeds as opposed to what is said, and what's recognized and celebrated (Yukl, 1998).

The hope for new principals is that they progress through both the anticipatory and encounter stages by the end of their first year so that they become "insiders" in the school. It isn't until this final period of transition that staff, students, parents, and community members finally accept the principal. Trusting and endearing relationships begin to form at this stage. As insiders, principals understand and respect the culture of the school, even as they may be working to reshape it. The speed with which beginners assimilate into the insider stage is directly linked to how well they fared in the encounter stage. Although principals might retain their position for several years, what largely determines their long-term success is the manner in which they are socialized into the school.

Like the Little Red Hen, newcomers bring a mixed bag of personal and professional experiences on their journey into the principalship. Personal background, such as cultural heritage, family relationships, gender, personality, and tolerance for change, coupled with their experiences as a teacher, university preparation, and previous administrative assignments, all influence principals' behavior. Rookies find their patience and confidence tested on a regular basis. They tend to take criticism and conflict personally. Running a school is a people business, and relationships are quite fragile during the transition period. Social and political maneuvering is necessary to navigate through the minefields in and around the schoolhouse.

Leadership Lessons in Emotional Intelligence

Few administrative functions in the principalship are carried out in isolation. As newcomers are socialized into the role, a major undertaking is to learn to take charge of their emotions before emotions take charge of them. Competent leaders rely on intuition to see the links among what they think, do, and say and are able to determine how their feelings affect their performance and relationships. To be respected, principals cannot keep people guessing about how they will react to a particular situation. Principals who demonstrate erratic dispositions don't last long in the job.

The qualities that distinguish the manner in which people regulate their feelings, interactions, and communication is commonly known as emotional intelligence (EI). Emotional intelligence is vital in any work setting but is paramount to survival in the principalship. Although the dimensions of emotional intelligence have existed for quite some time, it is only within the last decade that leading psychologists, such as Daniel Goleman, have uncovered the correlation of EI to individual and group performance. Goleman and other researchers believe that EI counts more than IQ (Pool, 1997).

Emotional intelligence functions as the pre-eminent barometer of achievement for school leaders.

Principals work vicariously through others to affect student learning. Setting academic expectations, serving as a resource for teachers, guiding improved teaching practices, promoting a vision that is shaped by parents and staff, and establishing systems to encourage parent involvement are the primary ways this is done (Gordon, 2003). To flourish in this role, principals have to "turn the mirror inward" and scrutinize the internal picture they hold of themselves (Senge, 1990, p. 9). This is known as intrapersonal intelligence (Goleman, 1995). In addition, principals need social savvy or interpersonal intelligence to correctly read the body language, tone, and facial expressions of others. Job demons that haunt first-timers, such as overload, isolation, and resistance to change can be exorcised once an internal locus of control is developed. In essence, new leaders have to accept the fact that any shortcomings—along with any strengths—are a manifestation of their own effort and motivation, not the result of external forces.

Through emotional conditioning, good administrators learn to remain even-keeled amidst a storm of daily chaos. They contour their responses to meet a range of constituent needs and interests. The five domains of emotional intelligence in Figure 4.1 outline the attributes that guide the thinking and actions of all principals. To strengthen each domain, rookies must learn to ask for feedback and take suggestions to heart.

To become more empathetic, for example, principals need to understand that their position holds tremendous symbolic power. An incident in my own district offers a poignant illustration. After a month on the job, a new principal began experiencing some hostility from teachers about her disregard for traffic problems in the parking lot. The principal was confused. She thought she was doing everything right by dutifully directing the flow of cars and cheerfully waving goodbye as parents pulled away from the school.

FIGURE 4.1
The Five Domains of Emotional Intelligence

Emotional Component	Definition	Attributes
Self-Awareness	The ability to recognize your emotions and the effects of your moods on other people; being aware of your strengths and weaknesses.	• Self-confidence • Open to feedback • Sense of humor • Reflective
Emotional Management	The ability to manage disruptive emotions and impulses (fear, anxiety, anger, sadness); thinking before you act; taking responsibility for your actions.	• Self-control • Trustworthiness • Adaptability • Innovation
Motivation	The ability to channel emotions into the service of a goal; remaining hopeful even when facing setbacks; seizing opportunities.	• Achievement driven • Optimism • Initiative
Empathy	The ability to sense others' perceptions and feelings; seeing what others need to bolster their ability; listening to and validating the concerns of others.	• Sensitivity and servitude • Appreciation for diversity • Political and social awareness
Relationship Management	The ability to understand the emotional fibers that make up others and to treat them accordingly; the ability to persuade, initiate change, and create group synergy.	• Good communication • Conflict management • Leadership • Building rapport

Adapted from the work of Daniel Goleman and the Consortium for Research on Emotional Intelligence in Organizations.

When the principal finally approached a teacher for advice, her error was revealed. Her predecessor had always greeted students where parents dropped them off in the mornings, but she was standing near the parents' exit. In the afternoon, the principal was expected to be at the parking lot exit; instead she was in the student loading area. Her choices of position slowed down the traffic pattern; once she repositioned herself, all was well. By looking inside herself, she was able to validate the feelings of teachers instead of minimizing them. We've even used the phrase "standing in the wrong place" to refer to situations that one of us has inadvertently misread. This profound "aha" helped the principal become more empathetic toward the feelings and concerns of others.

To measure your propensity to respond with a level head and effectively handle workplace issues, it may be interesting to use one or more of the emotional intelligence self-assessments available. The instrument developed by Nick Hall at www.saluminternational.com.htm is especially user-friendly. After beginning principals determine their emotional resiliency, they can sit down with a mentor, peer, or supervisor to create a plan for self-development. Keep in mind that emotional intelligence isn't just about professional success; it's about life success. By raising our EI, we all have the potential to become healthier, happier people.

Leading Beginners into the Zone

How does Lance Armstrong peddle faster, Tiger Woods perfect his swing, and Serena Williams dish up a fast-acing serve? Commitment, confidence, and control—all derivatives of EI—play a major part in the prowess of these athletes. To reach and sustain peak performance, however, world-class athletes also rely on the tutelage of a coach. Masterful coaches inspire people to "recognize the previously unseen possibilities that lay embedded in their existing circumstances" (Hargrove, 1995, p. 43). The goal for all top competitors is to have their best performance when it counts the most, therefore, skilled coaches work from the inside out to propel their protégés into the "zone," that special place where athletes weave a web of concentration and shut out all distractions. While in the zone, actions and decisions are effortless. Timing and tempo fit like a glove. Self-criticism is nonexistent. It is here that players take their game to the next level.

Finding the zone requires stamina, strength, and mental fitness— three things that novice principals have yet to perfect. Like an elite athlete, becoming an elite principal requires plenty of practice. Unfortunately, rookies have a tough time maximizing their potential because of the slew of mental barriers they face. Frequently, the novice principal's pattern of thinking prevents them from achieving breakthrough results. Gary Bloom from the New Teacher Center at the University of California, Santa Cruz, outlines 11 emotional conflicts commonly found among first-time principals:

1. Recognizing that they will be perceived and treated differently as a principal than they were as teachers.
2. Making the emotional leap from supervisor of students to supervisor of adults.
3. Learning to live under the spotlight; "celebrity status" requires giving up privacy and freedom.
4. Letting go of emotional responses to problems.
5. Giving up the need for perfection and control.
6. Accepting that the job is never finished.
7. Investing in their own well-being through the pursuit of interests and relationships outside of school.
8. Comfortably handling relationships with people in authority (superintendent, board, and high-level administrators).
9. Balancing relationships over productivity by keeping conversations short, yet still meeting the emotional needs of the other party.

10. Navigating unfamiliar landscapes with diverse clients to develop cultural sensitivity.
11. Not taking things personally. (Bloom, 2000, p. 34–39)

Intensive coaching and induction programs are the best ways to support a principal's early years. Formal coaching not only improves the retention rate for beginners, it catapults them through the transition period. According to Robert Hargrove, "Coaching is about interacting with people in a way that teaches them to produce often spectacular results in their businesses" (Hargrove, 1995, p. 1). A coach sees what others do not and then applies specific strategies to enhance his client's perceptions. Expanding this space of possibilities for rookie principals means it's only a matter of time before they, too, can experience the magic of the zone.

A Coaching Formula for Champions

As school districts explore coaching options, assistance should be targeted to lead new principals through the cultural, emotional, and political conflicts they encounter on a daily basis. Coaches go beyond the search for a quick fix by helping beginners see the difference between their intentions and actions. This is done through listening, observation, and inquiry. As a neutral party, a coach brings about personal transformation by

- examining how the principal conducts herself and treats others,
- determining whether the principal capitalizes on opportunities or shies away from them,
- identifying if the principal sees the difference between systemic and superficial causes of problems,
- recognizing the principal's ability to remain optimistic even in the face of adversity, and

- assessing the principal's level of emotional awareness. (New Teacher Center, 2002)

The New Administrator Program (NAP) at the University of California Santa Cruz has designed one of the most comprehensive coaching programs available to beginning principals. Since the program's inception in 1998, educators from the NAP have studied the needs and concerns of new principals to create a coaching formula for champions. Coaching Leaders to Attain Student Success (CLASS) is a nationally recognized training module that fosters effective principals through systematic induction and one-on-one support (New Teacher Center, 2002). The CLASS program is grounded in the following basic assumptions:

- New principals are not fully prepared to assume their duties without major support.
- Becoming an effective site principal is a developmental process.
- Effective coaching relationships are highly individual.
- New administrators do not necessarily know how to take advantage of coaching.
- Any program that supports new principals has to be respectful of the demands for time and attention already placed upon them by others in the organization.
- Coaches must be competent, trained, and available full time.
- The cost for such a program is insignificant when weighed against the real cost of failed leadership. (Bloom, 1999, p. 16–17)

The winning CLASS formula uses blended coaching techniques to teach new principals. Trained coaches guide clients by relying upon both instructional and facilitative strategies. Instructional coaching focuses on "showing and telling." In this method, the coach may provide direct advice, access to resources, or modeling of tasks.

Instructional techniques are best applied when the principal's needs are simple, operational in nature, and time-bound.

Facilitative coaching, on the other hand, is more sophisticated. The facilitative strategy is most appropriate when the novice has adequate background knowledge and experiences and there is a stronger chance for "prolific learning." In essence, the principal has to be able to recognize how his own assertions or biases are influencing a situation before he can modify his behavior. In the facilitative approach, the principal is molded into a reflective practitioner by looking beneath the surface for the causes of a problem, rather than focusing on the symptoms. Instead of proclaiming "Test scores are low in that class because the teacher is lazy," the principal is prompted to uncover what might be hindering the teacher's motivation. Facilitative coaching addresses issues related to the principal's emotional intelligence and disposition. Reducing a newcomer's natural tendency to become defensive or place blame on others when things don't go well is a prime example. As the coach poses clarifying questions, the principal discovers that talking less and listening more may change the outcome. This is transformational learning, which indisputably hastens the effect novices have on student learning. When the principal's observations and responses are grounded in data as opposed to assumptions, positive instructional changes are the obvious result.

The three-day CLASS workshop teaches prospective coaches how to identify and use each strategy with their new principals. Coaches learn about collecting data that is centered on induction research and principal needs. Log sheets, goal-setting forms, and toolkits are available to guide coaching conversations, build trusting relationships, and measure progress. The idea is for the coach to concentrate on immediate issues and concerns as well as on the principal's long-term professional development. Included in the CLASS training material are participation agreements and protocols to explain the program to the superintendent, faculty, colleagues, and parents. It's imperative that novice principals and key stakeholders clearly understand that the program is designed as a proficiency, not a deficiency, model. In other words, coaching is meant to sharpen a principal's inclination toward learning leadership, not correct performance deficits or concerns.

NAP recommends that coaches be available during the school day and that they come from outside the district. This guarantees confidentiality, ensures a neutral perspective, and prevents conflicts with the coach's time. Coaches are required to meet with first-year principals at least once every two weeks, and second-year principals every three weeks. A full-time coach is capable of working with as many as 20 first- and second-year principals, although 12 to 15 clients would be best.

As districts investigate the implementation of a coaching program for their new principals, the benefits should be weighed against the costs. Greater retention rates in the principalship, higher morale, and enhanced confidence all make for more effective principals. Tomorrow's champion principals will be those who are "mobilized into action" by constantly learning, adapting, and stretching goals to bring about real change (Hargrove, 1995, p. 89). It's impossible to have exemplary schools without exemplary leaders. First- and second-year principals deserve the chance to become exemplary leaders by training with a masterful coach. From Bacall to Baryshnikov, Pavarotti to Pacino, every great performer has a coach.

Building a Strong Base

Although coaching is undoubtedly the best formula to help novices develop into winners, valuable support systems can be installed to build a strong base. Buddy programs, mentoring, and principal academies provide additional cogs in the wheel of support.

As new principals come aboard, veteran principals can be enlisted to serve as buddies. A buddy's role is to give advice and encouragement on daily issues and problems. Outreach may come in the form of telephone conversations, e-mail correspondence, site visits, or job shadowing. Seasoned principals, who know the ins and outs of the district culture, are a great sounding board. They also have expertise in handling district protocol and procedures, which may be beyond the realm of an outside coach. Veterans regularly experience an increase in their own job satisfaction and leadership development as a result of working with a novice. Educators know that when we help someone learn, we often learn more than the person we're teaching. Buddy programs, then, are a two-for-one deal in enhancing principal effectiveness.

A central office mentor is another good resource to bolster support for a beginner. The ideal mentor is a former principal who works at the district office, but does not act in a supervisory capacity to the principal. District mentors can easily relate to the obstacles unwittingly imposed by the central office and have access to a network of people and inside information. Because most new principals are reluctant to call the central office for guidance, an assigned district mentor offers permission to do so in a safe, nonjudgmental context.

Having served in this capacity for four years, I can attest to the value of a district-level mentor. Simple suggestions like "The budget department is really busy working on the year-end report. How about if I go around the corner and check with them for you?" can mean a lot to a beginner. Helping new principals understand whom to call, when to call, and when not to call is invaluable. Providing this bridge to other departments significantly lowers newcomers' anxiety as they attempt to broaden their knowledge and experiences.

Finally, districts must actively endorse the participation of first-timers in principal academies and at state and national conferences. The Harvard Principal's Academy and other summer institutes for new and aspiring principals are an excellent way to affirm and rejuvenate beginners. Networking with others in similar

circumstances is reassuring to novices and helps them to put the job
in perspective. Academies also generate self-respect and recognition
for the work principals do. Chapter 5 examines ways of expanding
the professional competence and confidence of principals. By providing a new frame of reference, they may discover untried options
and choices. These fresh possibilities become the catalyst for new
skills, capabilities, and actions (Hargrove, 1995).

Champion athletes develop fitness and strength gradually. They
coax their bodies to handle greater stress with greater ease through
low-intensity workouts before applying anaerobic efforts. How
many runners attempt a marathon if their longest training distance
is only 10K? Coaches, buddies, mentors, and academies are ideal for
helping rookies develop and grow. The cornerstone of any successful
coaching program is to assist participants in building a strong confidence base to withstand the pressures of the principalship. The idea
is to lead the beginner into the zone for peak performance. Once
inside the zone, a spirit of triumph will prevail, as seemingly unob-
tainable tasks become manageable and easy.

Practical Principles for New Principals

Effective "principaling" calls for principled leadership. Maintaining
integrity and trustworthiness reaps tangible rewards. When trust is
present, the principal is treated as an insider and high-quality relationships blossom. When trust is absent, problems arise. It's not
what principals do that creates career-ending consequences, but
rather what they don't do. Poor interpersonal skills are the biggest
reason why principals fail in the job. Newcomers, then, must pay
careful attention to the perceptions of others and need regular feedback about how they are being perceived. Great sports heroes excel
not just because they possess exceptional physical attributes, but
because they avoid self-sabotage, heed the advice of others, and continually reinvent themselves. The competitors our society admires

most take things one step further by skillfully activating the talents of their teammates.

As beginners give rise to their winning combination of leadership, they must strengthen intrapersonal and interpersonal skills to galvanize their success during the induction period. Novices should concern themselves with doing the right thing instead of doing things right. Balancing technical competence against personal competence calls for common sense, emotional stability, and moral leadership. New principals need to be aware that sometimes the best intentions can have a negative affect on people—just as my colleague found out by standing in the wrong place to greet parents and students. What one person considers right, another may consider wrong. Therefore, principals have to constantly ponder the outcome of their actions.

Leadership emanates from a blend of personal attributes and characteristics. Transforming the learning and working conditions in a school through persuasion, fairness, and ethics is not an easy feat for any principal but is especially difficult for a rookie. To foster a positive and thriving school climate, these practical principles round out the playbook for first-year and second-year principals. Through practice and refinement, new principals will gradually begin to trust and believe in themselves.

- Never leave rules to chance.
  — Have clear and precise rules for adults as well as students.
- Refuse to be inconsistent.
  — Don't play favorites. Apply the rules fairly.
- Avoid the rumor mill.
  — Don't be sidetracked or misled by workplace gossip.
- Refuse to adopt a cynical attitude toward staff.
  — Take the high road and be an advocate for people when no one else will.

- Don't become defensive.
  — Remember you're not expected to know everything. Don't let yourself be backed into a corner trying to explain or justify a decision.
- Don't assume others will give you feedback.
  — Ask for feedback about your performance and let the staff know what you're working on.
- Never lose sight of the need to plan and organize.
  — Poor organization undermines your effectiveness. Adhere to time schedules, have agendas for meetings, and keep track of everything.
- Refuse to compromise quality.
  — Model the way by setting high standards. Expect the best from everyone, including yourself.
- Do not tolerate rude behavior from those who work in your office.
  — Front office staff set the tone for others. Demand courteous and sensitive behavior.
- Forget trying to do everything yourself.
  — Empower others to take responsibility and to make decisions. Learn to delegate!
- Avoid change simply for the sake of it.
  — Find what works well and build on it. Change only those things that detract from the school's mission and goals.
- Leave your previous school culture behind.
  — Don't try to transfer your old culture to your new school. Incorporate changes slowly.
- Be careful not to get carried away by the power of your position.
  — Keep in mind that leadership is exercised, not enthroned. (Lemley, et al., 1997)

The story of the Little Red Hen teaches us that first-timers often lack the self-assurance and wisdom to be top contenders in the principal's ring. The transition period for beginners is relatively short and imposes obstacles as the principal is socialized into the new role. Relationships between the principal and stakeholder groups are especially fragile during this initiation. Mental fortitude and emotional balance require deliberate support during a principal's first two years on the job. As rookies suit up for that big game we call the principalship, they must willingly accept guidance from coaches, peers, district mentors, and outside training sources. It takes time, practice, and endurance to reach the pinnacle of efficacy.

5

Helping Principals
Continue to Grow

Just when I'm ready to retire, I'm beginning to learn what this job
is all about.

—A principal after 33 years of service
Alvy & Robbins, 1998, p. 3

No matter how much a principal knows, there is always more to
learn. In our world of turbo-speed change, information is said to
double every seven years. Ten thousand scientific articles are published every day (Forman, 1995). The biggest problem facing modern-day society isn't a lack of progress, but rather an overabundance
of it. The most poignant example of this phenomenon involves Rus-
sian Cosmonaut Krikalev, who left Leningrad in 1991 for a 313-day
sojourn into space. When he returned almost a year later, he found
that his city was no longer on the map and his country no longer
existed (Blaydes, 1998, p. 27).

Principals are forever mired in shifting policies and reforms.
Unfortunately, each time a freshly hatched initiative comes along,
nothing is taken away. This saturation of stimuli weakens a leader's
immune system and causes what British psychologist David Lewis
calls "information fatigue syndrome" (Murray, 1998). In fact, a
worldwide survey in 1996 disclosed that 2 out of every 3 managers
suffer from increased tension and 1 out of 3 experience ill health
due to information overload (Heylighen, 1999). The saturation
means that principals are more likely to make poor decisions, be

forgetful, and have short attention spans. An increasing number are floundering as they attempt to juggle a multitude of responsibilities and learn new things in isolation. The frenetic pace of change and information in public education, let alone the world, is unlikely to slow, so principals are faced with the pain of growth or the pain of decay.

In *What's Worth Fighting For in the Principalship?* Michael Fullan surmises that most principals would rather play it safe than jump into the fray. The neon "tread lightly" sign that blinks above the front door of the central office aggravates that conservatism. Confronting an issue while others behave as if nothing is wrong can be risky business for a principal. Invisible hurdles give principals permission to either remain near the bottom of what their role allows or misinterpret what the system will condone. In this type of environment, it's easy for principals to become complacent. Fullan's argument is supported by the fact that school districts tolerate conflicting paradoxes among principals ranging from "passivity to activity, conformity to boldness, dullness to excitement, and incompetence to competence" (Fullan, 1997, p. 4). The behavior of boards, superintendents, and district office staff will either create the emergence of better schools and better leaders or perpetuate the status quo.

According to Malandro and Weiss (1999), there are three kinds of people in an organization—anchors, rafts, and speedboats. Think about the principals in your district. Their know-how and motivation probably spans many depths. Because of these variations, professional growth opportunities have to be carefully crafted to keep every leader fresh and adaptable. This can be accomplished by assessing the differing needs, assignments, and professional goals of each principal. To turn principals into speedboats, a culture of meaningful adult learning has to permeate the organization. If seasoned principals are to discover new lands, they must be willing to lose sight of the shoreline.

Thawing from the Big Freeze

As principals face simultaneous and sometimes polar changes, their experiences can be likened to the art of conducting an orchestra. Orchestra leaders have to keep track of various musicians, each playing a different instrument and note. As they gain a sense of the whole piece, conductors shift their attention from one section of the group to another. If there is no symphonic flow, every little transition sounds like "an unrelated melody that must be started and stopped without regard to the rest of the music" (Bridges, 1991, p. 71).

Principals view things differently from inside their orchestra pit. Personal history, assumptions, perceptions, and fears determine which way the baton is waved. How, then, can good principals be inspired to become seamless conductors as they deal with a barrage of new sheet music thrust upon them from outside the symphony hall? First, we need to understand how the dynamics of change affect a principal's behavior and performance.

Change can be both exhilarating and terrifying for principals. It brings a mixture of pleasure and pain as they come to terms with what's in and what's out. More than 50 years ago, Kurt Lewin theorized that as people contend with the elements of change, a sequence of events occurs. Lewin's "force-field" analogy aptly relates to the experiences of school leaders as new practices are introduced. Three overlapping stages define the psychological process principals are likely to encounter from the beginning of a change to its end: unfreezing, changing, and refreezing (Lewin in Yukl, 1998, p. 440). As one phase is exited, another is entered.

"Unfreezing" involves unlearning the old way. Principals begin to see that the manner in which they are doing something is no longer sufficient. Sometimes unfreezing occurs because of a crisis. For example: the superintendent leaves; enrollment radically declines; the school has failed to meet its performance target for a third year;

the district is taken over by the state. If principals are pushed into a change without unfreezing their attitudes and beliefs, apathy and resistance will result.

As principals start to thaw, "changing" begins. An implementation dip is evident as the change gestates. Given the ambiguity in this stage, some principals will rush forward while others lag behind to see if "this too shall pass." Anxiety can become quite high and motivation quite low during this state of flux. Conflict may also surface. District leaders can attempt to normalize things by seeking input on creative alternatives, insulating principals from further changes, revisiting the rulebook to see if policies and procedures can be modified, developing action research teams, breaking down the hierarchy and creating ad hoc groups to examine issues, and setting short-range goals to ensure small victories along the way. The lack of problem solving or absence of a vision for a promising future in the changing phase leads to a weak change plan (Yukl, 1998).

"Refreezing" is the final segment of the process, during which new approaches and systems start to take hold and become the norm. Old habits are replaced by different ways of doing business. Consensus and group cohesion solidify principals' enthusiasm and ensure a change has staying power. Repeated changes in a district, however, leave people less resilient. In other words, principals won't remain refrozen for long if they aren't protected, encouraged, and given a structure from which to work.

The Four C's of Logistical Leadership

If you don't know where you are going, you'll wind up somewhere else.

—*Yogi Berra*
(Stoddard, 2002, p. 1)

To scaffold continuous growth among a coalition of principals, district management has to model the way. Quite often, however, mandates from the top and the current reality at the bottom are disconnected. Because the design of most institutions, according to Richard Elmore (1999–2000, p. 8), professor at Harvard's Graduate School of Education, is one of "loose-coupling," the people heading the organization don't manage its basic functions. Rather, the "technical core" of instruction is left to teachers, who usually have little guidance or universal procedures for improving their practice (Elmore, 1999–2000, p. 8).

Today's preferred mechanism of central office oversight is one of "loose-tight coupling," suggesting that leaders are loose about some things and tight about others. In loose-tight structures, "closeness doesn't mean control and autonomy doesn't mean neglect" (Fullan, 1997, p. 43). Instead, the district's mission is crisp and clear while the freedom to develop shared values and goals to accomplish the mission is left up to the sites. Because student learning happens in the classroom, not in the central office, school boards, superintendents, and district administrators have to look honestly at how they might be contributing to a misaligned system. To determine district-wide progress, leaders need to study what's working, what's not, and why—at both the school level and central office level.

For school boards and superintendents to realize gainful improvements, governance must be redefined. The most progressive districts function like a global positioning system (GPS). Trustees and central office administrators monitor and signal from afar, yet remain a radar screen away when schools need guidance. Quality indicators of school board effectiveness include working to influence the policies of the legislative bodies whose decisions affect children, recognizing the difficulties of distinguishing policy from administration, and establishing and following protocols to govern its own functions (IEL, 2001, p. 19). In Texas, for instance, the law was rewritten to indicate that school boards "oversee" district operations, rather than "manage" them (IEL, 2001).

Gemberling and colleagues have outlined eight priority areas of board leadership (Gemberling et al., 2000). They place emphasis on developing a vision and systems of accountability in an environment that promotes ongoing improvement. Instead of stifling the work of schools, board members have to manage from the periphery. The guidebook includes self-assessment tools so trustees and superintendents can examine how they are doing. Of particular interest are side-by-side comparisons that delineate the different responsibilities of school board members and the superintendent in each priority area. Operational standards for school boards and accountability measures for meeting these standards ensure stability and success in a school district. Without a clear navigational system, all reform efforts are doomed.

If the central office hopes to provide guidance and support that will help and not hinder principals, it must practice loose-tight coupling via the four Cs of logistical leadership: clarity, capacity, coherence, and constancy (Houston, 2001, p. 46). The first C, clarity, implores the district office to establish a clear vision for the organization. Without a discernible purpose, new ideas are whimsical. For example, if the district's business is to invent high-quality work for students so that they learn more today than yesterday, then the vision has to frame the future that makes the work engaging and this learning possible. The goal is to get the herd heading north, although some schools may choose an alternate route to get there.

Capacity is the second C. It is the engine to get the work done. To accomplish goals, people need a tangible way to contribute and participate. The district office is supposed to act as resource central not command central. Distributed leadership calls upon district staff to share in the work rather than direct it. Daily missives such as "Where's the safety plan? How many second language learners do you have? Why is the monthly crime report late?" prevent principals from getting into classrooms and expanding leadership capacity among their staff. Principals have to be buffered from extraneous and distracting noninstructional issues, not showered by them.

The third C is coherence. No school is an island unto itself. Common expectations and a coherent set of values need firm roots in the organization. Collaborative relationships among and between schools and administrators must be promulgated. History reveals that great civilizations have risen to power by banding together to turn disadvantages into challenges that prompt creative solutions. After all, isn't that what America's founding fathers did? Coherence ties people together and instills a sense of control and purpose, no matter where they work.

In the final C, constancy, the central office guides schools in staying the course. Whatever happens this year has to connect to data from last year and link to what will occur next year. Change should be regarded as a "journey," not a "blueprint" (Fullan, 1997, p. 15). When managed effectively, the dynamics of change can lead to excitement and great destinations.

The absence of a coherent destiny leaves principals with few choices. They may (1) continue trying to do everything until they ultimately burn out, (2) draw their own possibly erroneous conclusions about what to do and what not to do, or (3) relinquish total control by constantly checking with superiors. If the central office is remiss about its obligation to help principals grow, leadership will be sporadic, haphazard, and minimal at best.

Making More Feel Like Less

To advance the development and resiliency of principals, conditions must be created so that more work actually feels like less. At the same time, internal capacity has to be built to sustain improvements within a school. Relationships between the central office and school sites should be one of "high engagement and low bureaucratization. High engagement means frequent communication, mutual coordination, and reciprocal influence [while] low bureaucratization [calls for] an absence of extensive rules and regulations governing the relationship" (Lambert, 1998, p. 87).

William Bridges (1991) identifies several pertinent techniques superintendents and key district leaders can use to keep principals from feeling as if they're caught inside the vortex of a tornado. Prudence and sensitivity will ensure that principals survive any sudden storms of change intact. Bridges's ideas are beholden to the premise that "before you can begin something new, you have to end what used to be" (Bridges, 1991, p. 19; for related discussion, pp. 24–80).

Postpone Extra Changes: Focus resources to make only those changes related to the major goals of the school. For example, it might not be a good year to introduce curriculum mapping if you are also launching a new teacher evaluation system. Be aware of the projects imposed by other departments and understand how these projects affect principals. Innovate judiciously.

Unload Old Baggage: Attempt to understand which principals are most affected by changes, legislative mandates, or new programs. Ask questions such as, "What's different from last year or the year before? What have you sacrificed or lost?" Recognizing principals' unresolved issues allows district leaders to set about healing any festering wounds.

Expect and Accept the Signs of Grieving: People often react to change the same way they react to traumatic and sad events in their life. Expect a range of grieving emotions among principals as old practices are laid to rest. Use ceremonies and rituals to allow principals to work through the responses of anger, denial, mourning, or disorientation. Once these feelings surface, look for ways to help principals adapt and compensate for their losses.

Treat the Past with Respect: Present ideas for change that build upon the district's current culture. Never ridicule the old ways because many veteran principals treasure them. Ask people who have been through similar changes to share their experiences with the group and explain how they were able to successfully manage the transition.

Sell Problems, Not Solutions: Make it clear to principals that there are serious problems that demand their attention; for example, students must meet the standards or outsiders will come in to run the school; the rising number of worker's compensation claims causing health and welfare premiums to soar; and special education encroachment is leading to fiscal insolvency. Problems are inevitable, so if principals are enlisted to help address them, solutions can be found more quickly. Inside every problem lurks an opportunity to learn and grow.

Do Worst-Case Scenarios: Develop "what if" questions and contingency plans. "What if the new high school doesn't open on time? What if seniors don't pass the high school exit exam? What if the newly adopted intervention program doesn't work?" This type of thinking provides administrators with alternate routes if the main arteries are closed.

Build Trust: When principals trust the superintendent, school board, and district managers, they're likely to embark upon new projects even if they are afraid of the outcome. When trust is absent, so too is the motivation for growth. Trustworthiness is built when supervisors do what they say they'll do, listen carefully, protect principals' interests, ask for feedback, and don't push principals to trust them any more than they are willing to trust the principals.

Give People Information Multiple Times: If principals don't have information, they'll make assumptions that may or may not be true. When it comes to dispersing information, superintendents sometimes fall into one of three traps: (1) They postpone telling principals things because they think giving the information later will cause less of a ruckus, (2) They figure principals already know about something because it was mentioned before, or (3) They believe not enough information is available to warrant passing it on to principals. Fabrications, misinformation, or no information all diminish trust within an organization.

Make the Transition to "Change as the Norm": Support principals in adopting a new mindset that change is mandatory for growth. This doesn't mean that change should be initiated simply for the sake of change. Not everything needs changing. However, "change as the norm" implies that school leaders must continually seek ways to raise achievement. Because learning is an ongoing process, it's unacceptable to assume students—or adults—have met their learning quota. Change only ends when we do, so we might as well get used to it.

Mark the Endings: Superintendents and their teams should let principals know what's really over by creating dramatic actions that mark the end of an era. If a district wants to change the context of its principals' meetings from a laundry list of minutia to meaningful dialogue, how about distributing a blank agenda every other month? A decisive act to facilitate two-way communication is the best way to make a point.

The most blatant example of a historical figure using this technique is the Spanish conquistador Cortés. After landing in Veracruz, Mexico, he found his sailors fearful and ambivalent as they faced a continent full of adversaries. With few options available, Cortés decided to burn the ships (Bridges, 1991, p. 29). Symbolic actions—not dangerous ones, of course—such as reorganizing a department or reducing layers of bureaucracy convince principals that it's time to move on. Seeing is believing.

People resist change for many reasons, from a lack of trust to the belief that the change isn't necessary or feasible, to the fear of personal failure or loss of power, to resentment of interference, or a threat to values and ideals. For advancing school districts to maintain an aura of growth throughout their organization, superintendents and boards have to instill balance and tranquility in the foundation. When principals and teachers find themselves constantly on the rebound of failed reforms, they become reluctant travelers. And reluctant travelers like to play it safe by not venturing too far from home. Reasonably clear and consistent communication, coordinated efforts, and mutual influence will actually make more feel like less. The power to make positive changes is in the hands of district leaders, not at the state capitol or inside the White House.

Principals as Lead Learners

With so much to know, learn, and do, it's no wonder principals' heads are spinning every time they return from a meeting or inservice training. In many districts, administrator training is reduced to a three-hour crash course on the latest innovation, contemporary issue, or state mandate. When district leaders want schools to be more collaborative, we throw the team-building manual at principals. When we expect principals to use data, we inundate them with test results with no training on how to classify, organize, or interpret the information. When a toxic culture prevails in a school, we remand the principal to a workshop on conflict management. When it comes to the learning of principals, training often centers on quick fixes and watered-down methodology. Somehow, there's never enough time to do it right, but there's always enough time to do it over.

Not only do school districts have an abysmal track record of reinforcing the concept of principals as "lead learners," Roland Barth (1990) concludes, but principals themselves are reluctant when it comes to spending time on their own professional growth. By nature, principals are people of action, not necessarily people of thought. "As learners, [they] have a bad reputation" (Barth, 1990, p. 68). The most common excuse we hear is lack of time. With the workday hovering at or beyond 11 hours, many principals argue that they cannot afford to be away from their campuses. And if they are, they believe they're punished for it when they return to a myriad of mechanical problems necessitating hours of repair.

Another impediment has to do with principals' prior experiences and attitudes toward learning. Veterans often build up resistance against attempts to be helped. Previous inservice training sessions have left them unsatisfied and cynical. Even if there is relevance to a topic, many principals are convinced there isn't. This self-fulfilling prophecy hinders the replenishment of knowledge into the principalship.

A third drawback involves the belief held by many principals that it is inappropriate to use taxpayers' dollars for their own personal learning. As public servants they see their duty is to give, not take, from the coffers of students. Sadly, this view is all too often maintained by parents and teachers, who think the principal belongs in the schoolhouse administering to the needs of the congregation.

Finally, if principals attend training and actually learn something new, they will be expected to use it. In other words, they are rewarded for their efforts by creating more work for themselves. With time already in short supply, this means the principal will get further behind.

Taking a stand to sustain the professional growth and self-worth of principals requires the central office to practice what it preaches. In my own school district, for instance, constancy and coherence is provided through a professional development series that has spanned the last five years. Principals, coadministrators, and every manager from the instruction division reach for the STARs via theme-based sessions tied to Standards, Teamwork, Assessment, and Results. People who understand the needs and hesitations of principals use districtwide achievement data to plan workshops. Clarity is spawned through integrated sessions such as Working as a Professional Learning Community, Understanding What to Do with Data, Writing SMART (Specific, Measurable, Attainable, Results-driven, Time-bound) Goals, Recognizing Standards-based Instruction When

You See It, Conducting Effective Teacher Evaluation Conferences, and Curriculum Mapping. Leadership toolkits are distributed for administrators to use with their staffs so that they can immediately implement what's been gleaned from each monthly session.

Ignoring the progress of principals causes stagnation and perpetuates a climate of decay in our schools. Leading to learn is as critical for a principal as learning to lead. To instigate substantive growth in the principalship, the Interstate School Leaders Licensure Consortium (ISLLC) has outlined overarching standards that drive the learning of administrators (Council of Chief State Schools Officers, 1996). Thirty-five states and nearly every educational organization have embraced the ISLLC standards, or derivatives of these standards, which serve as the platform for reinventing the role of school leaders. From redesigning university preparation programs to revamping the professional development and evaluation of principals, the ISLLC standards are the meat and potatoes for improving schools from the inside out (see Figure 5.1). Charting a realistic path for principals to achieve these standards creates clarity, capacity, coherence, and constancy within school systems. This in turn makes the focus of the entire educational community all the more potent.

Sharpening the Saw Through Vision, Values, and Voice

The ISLLC standards call upon school administrators to work as stewards, designers, and teachers in promoting the success of all students. As a steward, the principal oversees the larger purpose of the school and guides the vision. The emphasis is to make a measurable difference in the lives of children. As a designer, the principal sculpts the learning process by infusing core values into the foundation of the school. Attitudes and traditions are transformed into supportive, as opposed to subversive, practices. An aura of energy and enthusiasm spills from the hallways. The principal as teacher

---

FIGURE 5.1
ISLLC Standards for School Leadership

A school administrator is an educational leader who promotes the success of all students by

Standard 1: Facilitating the development, articulation, implementation, and stewardship of a vision of learning that is shared and supported by the school community.

Standard 2: Advocating, nurturing, and sustaining a school culture and instructional program conducive to student learning and staff professional growth.

Standard 3: Ensuring management of the organization, operations, and resources for a safe, efficient, and effective learning environment.

Standard 4: Collaborating with families and community members, responding to the diverse community interests and needs, and mobilizing community resources.

Standard 5: Acting with integrity and fairness, and in an ethical manner.

Standard 6: Understanding, responding to, and influencing the larger political, social, economic, legal, and cultural context.

Source: Council of Chief School Officers, 1996.

---

mobilizes the environment and conveys insight through compassion and voice. Leading adults through a service orientation breeds hope and inspiration among staff. To construct meaningful change, experienced principals need to sharpen their saws through the conscious expression of vision, values, and voice.

Principals can begin their stewardship by asking, "What kind of school do we hope to become?" A school's vision should speak to people. To do so, it has to be genuine, research-based, and used as the blueprint for improvement. Dynamic principals visualize what the end product will look like and know what needs to be done to achieve it. An image emerges as the principal identifies ideas with wide appeal, listens to staff to decide which traditions should be maintained, links the present with the future, focuses on process over product, and continually assesses the dreams and aspirations of the collective group.

To set the vision-shaping process in motion, the principal might ask the faculty to examine the present reality (i.e., What is happening now in our building?) in relation to their ideals for the future (i.e., Where do we want to be in 5 years?). Rating a variety of statements in terms of how well they describe the conditions in the school allows teachers to ponder these important questions. Survey statements might include

- Our school is organized to respond to the needs and interests of students.
- Teachers believe their job is to teach and the students' job is to learn.
- There is typically no uniform school curriculum as subjects are taught in isolation.
- The school has no infrastructure to support teacher collaboration.

A summary of staff responses to these and other statements can lay the groundwork for an emerging vision. The Planning Worksheet: Vision for School Improvement (Appendix B) is a tool for stimulating further discussion. After grade level or departmental visions take shape, the principal and leadership team should use all the input to create a schoolwide vision. The litmus test lies not in the vision statement itself, but in the directional force it provides the school. When a principal underestimates or ignores the power of vision, there is no synergy between the picture of the future and the current reality.

Values and norms define how a school operates on a daily basis as people grapple with critical issues. A school's core values come from the mental models of the employees who work there. Mental models are "deeply ingrained assumptions, generalizations or images" that determine how people interpret and react to things (Senge, 1990, p. 8). In any given situation, we can all behave differently if we change our mental model. Principals work as designers by surfacing and improving others' internal pictures of how the world operates or reshaping the way a circumstance is perceived. When teachers are exposed to such learning and growing conversations, it fosters good will among colleagues, encourages professional behavior, and builds a loyal team.

In their book *In Search of Excellence,* Peters and Waterman (1982) noted that every standout company they studied was driven by a coherent value system and took the process of "value shaping" quite seriously. They found that the esprit de corps of an organization was far more responsible for its achievements than technological advances, economic resources, innovation, or company structure. Furthermore, the leaders of these successful companies were described as "implementers par excellence" (Peters & Waterman, 1982, p. 288).

As head designer, the principal is responsible for ensuring core values are articulated and followed. This is accomplished by recognizing the best role models in the school, observing rituals that sanctify important beliefs, and staging value-laden traditions and ceremonies throughout the year (Deal & Peterson, 1999). Shared values "represent the essential ABC's of school improvement because [they] challenge the people within that organization to identify the specific attitudes, behaviors, and commitments they must demonstrate in order to advance toward their vision" (DuFour & Eaker, 1998, p. 88). Figure 5.2 exemplifies purposeful faculty values in both elementary and secondary school settings. Without ideals that bind the faculty together, the values are reduced to a meaningless list donning the hallways.

The most talented principals influence through voice. What is said, how it is said, and the examples that are set tell the educational community much about a leader. As teachers themselves, principals use tone, stories, and humor to convey compassion, integrity, fairness, and inspiration. According to Sally Helgesen (1990), author of *The Female Advantage: Women's Ways of Leadership,* voice is much more than a vocal instrument. Voice is a way to send powerful messages through subtlety and sensibility. A vision might

FIGURE 5.2

Shared Values—Elementary and Secondary Schools

Elementary School	Secondary School
We will identify the essential outcomes of each grade level and help each student achieve those outcomes.	We will teach to the agreed-upon objectives and provide evidence of student achievement in those objectives.
We will teach for understanding, frequently assessing students' understanding.	We will help all students achieve the intended outcomes of the curriculum by addressing their individual needs and learning styles.
We will provide a variety of ways for students to demonstrate mastery.	We will make full use of instructional time.
We will work collaboratively to develop instructional strategies, design assessment methods, and advance the vision of the school.	We will collaborate with one another and our students to achieve our collective goals more effectively.
We will provide an inviting classroom environment with clear expectations, consistent consequences, and specific academic goals.	We will help ensure an orderly atmosphere that is conducive to learning throughout the building.
We will involve the parents and community at-large in the learning process by creating shared learning experiences.	We will demonstrate our commitment to ongoing professional development and continuous improvement.
We will model the lifelong learning and commitment to high-quality work that we hope to develop in our students.	We will promote a positive school climate by modeling the qualities and characteristics that we hope to instill in our students.
We will monitor the results of our individual and collective efforts and use evidence of results to guide our continuous improvement.	We will involve parents in the education of their children by keeping them informed of student progress and offering suggestions for assisting their students.

Richard DuFour & Robert Eaker. (1998). *Professional Learning Communities at Work* (pp. 90–91). Bloomington, IN: National Educational Service.

exist on its own, even if it's not communicated. But to use voice, says Helgesen, someone has to be there to hear it, to listen, and respond. Voice finds its form through interaction and inclusion (Helgesen, 1990, p. 223). Without this level of spontaneous expression, a principal's voice rings flat and untrue.

A compelling example of a leader who inspired through voice comes from a World War II story (Yukl, 1998). Two months after the bombing of Pearl Harbor, Lt. Col. Evans Carlson faced 1,000 eager Marine recruits at a San Diego training base. Frustrated by the lack of communication between commanders and subordinates, Lt. Col. Carlson told the men that it was a contradiction to have such an "undemocratic military" in our democratic society. In this new unit, he planned to maintain discipline based upon reason rather than blind obedience. Carlson went on to say that he and his officers would have no special privileges, would eat and sleep with the men, would issue no unnecessary orders, and would not require any needless saluting. The troops stirred as they heard this anathema to centuries-old military traditions.

Carlson proceeded to describe how the training would be structured. Marching 50 miles a day with little food or rest was to become the standard. To make the looming hardships and danger bearable, he suggested that the battalion, dubbed the Raiders, adopt the principles the Chinese had so successfully used against Japanese invaders. The Chinese had accomplished remarkable feats through attitude, confidence, and motivation. Chinese soldiers, according to Carlson, respected one another and worked together without "fear or favor." He went on to promise that he and his officers would do their part by taking up arms with the men and making sure they understood the importance and purpose of each battle.

To conclude his speech, Lt. Col. Carlson explained to the Marine Raiders that the Chinese had two words for working together: "gung" meaning work and "ho" meaning harmony. "Gung ho," he said, would give them all the chance to practice the democracy that embodied

American ideals. After proposing that the slogan represent the spirit of the battalion, Carlson shouted in a booming voice, "Gung Ho. Let's hear you [boys] say it." A brief pause ensued before the crowd of eager Marines belted in unison this strange foreign phrase that was to become as American as apple pie (Yukl, 1998, pp. 462–463).

Through voice, Lt. Col. Carlson taught his men how to band together and fight with dignity and honor. He also helped them dig deep within themselves to find the courage they needed to prove to the Japanese that America was a force to be reckoned with.

Full-Circle Performance Review

To maintain gung ho vitality in your school district, a meaningful process for employee appraisal and feedback has to be firmly embedded in the culture. The days of unilateral supervisor-subordinate performance evaluations are going by the wayside in the corporate United States; however, progress in educational circles is spotty. Despite some headway in the use of more authentic teacher evaluations, the notion of performance-based assessment for administrators has yet to take hold.

Multirater, or 360-degree feedback, may be the key to principal transformation in your organization. Done correctly, a 360-degree principal appraisal system is a valid and reliable means to judge a leader's performance. Furthermore, it can be used at three levels: (1) for developmental purposes—for employees' eyes only; (2) for evaluation; and (3) for compensation (Manatt, 2000, p. 10). A key benefit of 360-degree feedback is that it corrals a range of stakeholder feedback. This produces a broader and more complete picture of how principals are doing and whether they are improving each year (Milliman, et al., 1994).

The concept behind multirater feedback is to have the people who regularly deal with the principal formulate a pool of information and perspectives about how that principal is performing. When superintendents or other supervisors use conventional approaches to evaluate principals, either the data aren't adequate to hold anyone accountable or every principal ends up with the same rating. More often than not, these similar ratings are woefully inflated because the supervisor lacks concrete evidence to measure the principal's true performance.

Full-circle principal performance review requires deliberate and careful planning by the school district. To garner constructive feedback and generate support for the process, organizational maturity is necessary. Hasty implementation or shortcuts will damage morale and intimidate principals. Therefore, moving slowly with the gradual introduction of 360-degree feedback is the safest way to begin. A three-year implementation cycle is ideal. This might include a small year-one pilot group consisting of experienced principals who volunteer to participate. Only five or six data sources may be used. In year two, a larger, more representative group of principals can be involved using all data sources except parent feedback. By year three, every principal and all data sources should be a part of the process (Manatt, 2000).

The College of Education at Iowa State University has worked for the past several years developing sample instruments, conducting norming studies, processing and analyzing data, and establishing benchmarks to define school leader effectiveness. Although the methods to acquaint principals with the concept of multirater feedback will vary from district to district, leading experts in 360-degree feedback propose several universal steps as a guide:

1.   Determine administrator readiness for 360-degree feedback.
     • Assess whether enough trust exists between the supervisor and principals to introduce the process.
     • Help principals understand what 360-degree feedback is and how it works.
     • Decide how confidentiality and fairness will be practiced.

2. Develop appropriate survey instruments based upon principals' needs, state leadership standards, and district objectives.
   - Use a team of principals and managers to design the appraisal criteria and format.
   - Align survey items with the district's mission and desired outcomes.
   - Explore the possibility of using an outside source, such as Iowa State University, for survey design and scoring. An outside source will ensure the inclusion of reliability measures and item discrimination.

3. Create a sampling procedure that fits your district's needs.
   - Determine who will be asked to provide feedback and how many respondents will be targeted in each category. The most effective 360-degree appraisals elicit feedback from both internal and external clients.
   - Consider the following multiple sources of feedback to assess principals:
     —Supervisor evaluation
     —Self-evaluation
     —Student achievement information
     —Student feedback
     —Student attendance
     —Teacher performance data
     —Teacher feedback
     —Parent feedback
     —Holding power (dropout rate; mobility)
     —School climate survey

4. Ensure participants and respondents have the skills to support the process.
   - Provide respondents and supervisors with training on how to offer constructive feedback.

- Provide principals with the skills and training necessary to accept feedback and effectively manage their performance.

5. Administer the surveys.
    - Surveys can be distributed and collected online, in scantron form, via telephone, or by mail.
    - Attempt to keep the raters' identities anonymous to avoid the fear of retribution from teachers and parents. Confidentiality should prevail.

6. Validate the results.
    - Use an outside authority to compile the data, check for validity, and analyze the results.

7. Provide an organizational summary for the superintendent and board.
    - Evaluate trends and patterns among principals as a whole, by level, and by other useful categories (low or high performing schools; male vs. female; years of experience).
    - Exercise caution when a single rater has given highly negative or highly positive feedback.

8. Use feedback for improvement.
    - Have the superintendent or supervisor meet with principals individually or in small groups to examine strengths and shortcomings.
    - Jointly develop performance goals and action steps for the upcoming evaluation cycle.

9. Publicize good examples after the process has been field-tested.
    - It's important for principals to realize the information has validity and is taken seriously. Positive results can be

publicized in the local newspaper, on the district's Web site, and in school newsletters.

10. Readminister the survey the following year.
    - Once baseline information is established, progress should be measured against this data. The process must be ongoing for principals to experience continuous growth and to recognize that their performance evaluation is not a hit-or-miss endeavor. (Manatt, 2000; Team Builders Plus, 2002)

Keep in mind that 360-degree feedback is a sampling technique and not an all-inclusive rating system. The ability to objectively receive feedback is as important for principals as being able to give feedback. If principals don't accept constructive input well, people won't offer it. With the right training and implementation strategy, incentives and recognition can be tied to appraisal results, which in turn will motivate and renew principals.

Closing the Learning Gap for Leaders

School districts are under pressure to retool the knowledge and skills of principals amid gale-force changes. Cutting-edge professional development cannot be limited to hit-or-miss inservice training. By focusing only on training content, critical factors that influence learning such as motivation, confidence to learn, audience experience, and learning style all get overlooked. Therefore, time to collaborate and reflect with colleagues must be incorporated into the learning process. Without use and practice, people forget 25 percent of what they hear in six hours, and 33 percent within 24 hours (Sage Learning Systems, 2001). School districts must help principals investigate how their leadership skills impact student learning and give them an array of opportunities to assess their own professional growth. Practicing administrators need to rely upon a multitude of feedback and data sources to set improvement goals conjoined with peaks, not valleys. The age of accountability isn't just for teachers and students. Because principals foster the climate in which students and teachers ultimately succeed or fail, improving the principal's learning provides leverage in making systemic changes geared to raise student achievement.

It takes a crew working together to stay afloat on the waters of reform. Sustainability in schools depends upon many learning leaders. Districts owe it to their clients to guarantee that every principal meets and maintains high standards of performance and commits to the continuous study of making schools even better. The chance for principals to learn on the job and learn from peers reduces the pain of growth to nothing more than a minor malady, hardly noticeable as they sail along the towering seas. With a good navigational system and a strong group of sailors, principals can rest assured they'll return to shore safely.

6

Keeping Good Leaders

Don't expect to build up the weak by pulling down the strong.

—*Calvin Coolidge*

As the Industrial Revolution swept across the Atlantic near the turn of the 20th century, the nature of work in the United States experienced drastic changes. Business leaders and government officials turned their attention to the domestic labor force with the hope of finding one best system in which tasks could be completed and organizational problems could be solved. Scientists and engineers, including Frederick Winslow Taylor, purported that if supervisors divided jobs into smaller parts and planned a worker's daily schedule from start to finish, production could be closely scrutinized. Consequently, more cost-efficient ways of doing things would be discovered. The model called for an autocratic, hierarchical structure due to the belief that employees themselves possessed little motivation. The assembly line concept, conceived from Taylor's principals, left no room for alterations and paid little attention to the human side of an enterprise (Townley, et al., 1999, p. 2–3). Leading educators of the day embraced Taylor's thinking and argued that schools should adopt his model to produce the type of workers industry needed. In the late 1890s, Superintendent and National Education Association President William T. Harris wrote:

> Our schools are in a sense, factories, in which the raw materials (children) are to be shaped and fashioned in order to meet the various

demands of life. The specifications for manufacturing come from the demands of the 20th century civilization, and it is the business of the school to build its pupils according to the specifications laid down. (DuFour & Eaker, 1998, p. 21)

Although these ideals are harsh by today's standards, they shed light on the entrenched foundation of our educational system. Principals were assigned to schools solely to manage the plant and ensure uniformity of the curriculum. Since schools were not expected to educate large numbers of students to a particularly high level, the factory model of schooling was quite sufficient at the time. Sadly, many educators have been slow to adapt to any rudimentary changes in the infrastructure of the schoolhouse. Yet it is widely recognized that contemporary schools and their principals, now under the auspices of accountability, must be original, flexible, and innovative to meet the needs of such a diverse and sophisticated clientele (Murphy & Doyle, 2001).

Throughout the last century, social scientists expanded their studies of U.S. workers to determine the essence of employee motivation and to identify what gave a company holding power. Although each decade spawned new revelations, the research is grounded in the notion that organizations can't survive without paying attention to their human capital. Study after study reveals that employee retention in any industry is intricately tied to recruitment practices and on-the-job relationships. Even today, workers say that they value involvement and recognition over salary and wages. Appreciation for the job done, feeling "in" on things, and an employer's sympathetic understanding of personal problems are the three things people desire most from their position (Hersey & Blanchard, 1988, p. 48). Although money is certainly necessary, it's not a sufficient condition to attract, retain, and motivate good staff. Notice the energy and enthusiasm of many volunteers in your own school district and community. The secret is to pay employees fairly, but to treat them incredibly well.

Becoming a Great Place to Work

Once a school district has grown its own good leaders, it must find
ways to keep them. The reputation of a district and how people feel
about working there is the most influential recruitment and retention factor (Basom, 2002). If people perceive a district or particular
school as a winner, they are more likely to feel a strong desire to be
affiliated with it. Applicants flock to these places in droves. Then, if
districts are selective about whom they hire, there's a better chance
of establishing the ideal fit between employees and the organization. A good match means people are more likely to stay. The easiest
way to hold on to high-quality principals is to ensure that the
school district is a great place to work. After all, winners like to "up
the ante, raise standards, and conquer the next mountain" (Kouzes
& Posner, 1987, p. 253).

A 1998 Gallup survey found that satisfied employees propagate
positive attitudes. Above-average attitudes parlayed into 38 percent
higher customer satisfaction scores, 22 percent higher productivity
ratings, and 27 percent higher profits (Grimme, 2001, p. 2). The
survey confirmed that people are drawn to successful companies by
stimulating work as well as the relationships formed while the work
gets done.

Public institutions are no different when employee engagement is
compared to education's bottom line: student achievement. If your
school district isn't already an employer of choice, consider these
strategies adapted from Basom (2002) to become one:

Organize Your District as a Learning Community: Provide time
and space for practitioners to talk about their craft. A learning community is a place where people constantly seek ways to create a
better future together. Being part of a learning community means
being part of something larger than yourself. Learning communities
stimulate cohesion and inclusion.

Train Supervisors to Identify True Talent: Instead of looking for things principals don't do well, the superintendent and senior staff must concentrate on talent. Employees bring their own motivation with them to work, and outstanding leaders capitalize on this by seeing the strength and potential in others. Poor leaders rarely notice such things because they are too busy scrutinizing people's weaknesses. "Leadership is the liberation of talent, rather than restraint by rule" (Peters & Austin, 1985, p. 239).

Don't Be Afraid to Build Relationships: Don Clifton, chair and chief executive officer of Gallup's Selection-Research Division, purports that relationships are not inconsequential to a company's outcomes. In fact, says Clifton, as relationships improve, the benefits increase geometrically. The primary reason that people cite for leaving a job is they believe no one cares about them. Conversely, when employees feel valued and get along with their bosses, these positive feelings enhance attendance, retention, quality of service, and productivity (Clifton & Nelson, 1992, p. 141).

Celebrate Milestones and Successes: If you want to improve the performance of principals, applaud them for good work. Eighty-two percent of those polled in the Gallup survey agreed that recognition inspires them to improve performance (Wolfe, 1998, p. 1). Everyone enjoys accolades. The key is to find out how your administrators like it served. Whether it is public or private, a written note, verbal compliments, enhanced responsibilities, promotions, perks, or other incentives, recognition must be tailored to individual desires and needs. Remember Mark Twain's words, "I can live two months on a good compliment"?

Maintain a Clear Focus: Once the mission and purpose of your district are developed, be sure the principals understand what is personally expected of them. The goals of an organization should be linked with the professional goals of the individuals in it. Determine what people do well, and use your mission to drive and unify them. The absence of a clear purpose or inconsistent expectations prevents leaders from capitalizing on their own strengths as well as the strengths of subordinates.

Help Principals Experience a Sense of Achievement: Principals need to feel as if they make a difference in their workplace. When they do, they naturally look forward to coming to work. Striking a balance between expectations, relationships, strengths, and recognition stimulates an electric atmosphere in a school district. Achievements, both large and small, should be praised promptly, sincerely, and at a rate four times higher than mistakes. Sharing the credit with principals generates excitement and adds to the drive toward results (Basom, 2002).

Perhaps your place of employment already exemplifies some of these characteristics. Several examples of effective administrator-retention practices are being used in school districts, but for the most part they appear to be the exception rather than the rule (Quinn, 2002). Given the superhuman expectations foisted upon our 21st-century principals, finding and keeping strong leaders presents a challenge. Yet, maintaining a vibrant work environment for principals is vital to a district's longevity. In the wake of looming retirements, diminishing applicant pools, declining employee loyalty, and budget-induced downsizing, survival depends upon holding on to the leaders you already have. It's the district leaders' obligation to do whatever they can to boost and retain principals in their own backyard.

Principal Gratification Equals an Invitation to Stay

Principals play such a pivotal role in driving teaching and learning in our schools that taking care of them isn't just the cordial thing to do, it's the only thing to do. Ensuring that they feel valued and important is a sure-fire ingredient to hold on to them. Principal gratification comes from decision-making freedom and the power to do what's expected, networking with peers to share information and learn best practices, fair and reasonable systems of accountability, and validation for a job well done. This support not only provides an invitation to remain in the profession, but yields high-quality leadership through the process.

A school district can construct specific experiences to enhance principal gratification and fortify the "leadership pipeline." The following collection of ideas comes from districts across the United States. Improving principal retention rates doesn't take money but does require a little effort. To make something happen in your workplace, consider implementing a few of these tried-and-true techniques.

All in the Family

Medium and large school districts commonly suffer from impersonal and disjointed structures. The mammoth Los Angeles Unified School District (LAUSD), for example, has 677 schools serving more than 736,000 students sprawled over 704 square miles. To create "a critical mass of restructured schools," a group of 249 campuses came together in 1995 through the Annenberg Challenge, a national reform initiative to improve student achievement. Twenty-eight school "families" were formed, each comprising five to nine sites. Family networks typically include a high school and its feeder elementary and middle units. The LAUSD school families make decisions through three distinct teams: management, integration, and improvement. Management teams provide direction and oversight, integrating teams coordinate activities across the network, and improvement teams focus on making changes that have an impact on teaching and learning. Team membership consists of cross-representation from the participating schools. The integrating team is primarily made up of principals, while the improvement team is a mixture of administrators and teachers. Management team membership runs the gamut of administrators, teachers, parents, and classified staff. Governance occurs through the management team, which acts upon recommendations from the other groups and operates much like a site council (Wohlstetter & Smith, 2000).

Family coordinators, usually a principal from each cohort, were originally designated to manage the network. Over time, the role proved to be too much for principals, who were already knee-deep in running their own schools. In response, many families earmarked funds to hire a full- or part-time facilitator. Facilitators now provide general oversight of the Annenberg grant and serve as the network manager. They centralize administrative functions and facilitate operational procedures like scheduling meetings, planning joint activities, sharing information, and tracking expenditures. Another important responsibility of the facilitator is to serve as a "broker" in communicating up and down the hierarchy. The conduit is especially valuable when authority is unclear and family decisions conflict with the philosophies of the upper echelon.

Family structures are a strategic way to organize principals into a learning community. Meetings might focus on standards-based instructional practices, data analysis, curriculum development, and community issues. Bringing groups of educators together to work on behalf of every child who matriculates through their school network leads to vertical alignment. Such collective responsibility enhances the overall capacity of the participating schools to support change, share resources, and promote a culture of adult and student learning.

Tell District Leaders What You Think

As previously noted, open communication and feeling included are important to employees. Yet more often than not, principals are on the receiving end of directives and mandates over which they have no input or control. As the persons responsible for seeing these measures through, principals find it disconcerting to experience full accountability with little or no involvement or authority.

To keep principals in the loop and to tap their knowledge, the central office should take time to ask them what they think. Two avenues in which principals can safely share their opinions, ideas, and concerns are focus groups and area meetings. Focus, or ad hoc groups, are made up of five to eight principals with mixed expertise. The group is brought together to provide input and suggestions before the district moves forward with an idea. In this intimate setting, principals are able to be candid about their thoughts and reservations. Successful companies test market new products before moving into mass production. Principal focus groups, then, make good business sense by giving the central office solid information to consider before proceeding with full-blown implementation of a proposal.

Area meetings, on the other hand, provide a venue for principals to meet by region and levels (elementary, middle, and high school) to problem solve and reflect on current issues. The group examines programs or policies that are already under way but seem to be causing discomfort. When things are swept under the carpet, they turn into the elephant that everyone tries to ignore. As long as the elephant remains on the table, the real meal can't be served. Area meetings are designed to get the elephant off the table and back into the zoo. Then the group can set about fixing problems by addressing the deeper concerns that are obstructing progress.

Programs, procedures, and innovations cannot successfully be imposed in schools without principals on board, so it makes sense to talk to them first. To truly influence job satisfaction, however, the suggestions principals offer must be heeded. If most of their recommendations are ignored, principals will come to realize that asking for their opinion is nothing more than smoke and mirrors.

Keep It Simple

As discussed in Chapter 5, the age of information has arrived and is here to stay. In 2002, the number of e-mail messages passing through the Internet was 31 billion. By 2006, that number is expected to rise to 60 billion per year (Le, 2003, p. 30). No one is immune to the daily barrage of memos, faxes, advertisements, journals, spam, and e-mail messages reaching our desk at mach-10 speed. It may seem insignificant, but by understanding how principals process information and by finding ways to help them sift through the "data smog" (Murray, 1998), districts can increase principals' job satisfaction. The key to effective communication is to keep it simple.

Principals' decisions are affected by an overabundance of information from higher levels of administration. Data overload fuels disorganization, wastes time, and drains a principal's energy. Keeping up with the deluge triggers stress, frustration, and irritability, which can ultimately cause burnout and serious illnesses. To reduce the onslaught of paperwork and out-of-control e-mail messages, someone at the central office needs to monitor the message flow to schools. In a single hour a principal may be inundated with 10 directives from different departments who are oblivious to the demands from the other departments and clients. E-mail is both a blessing and a curse as expectations of immediacy are attached to each message. To insulate principals from the rising volume of electronic messaging, the central office must find a means to manage information before it manages principals. Capistrano Unified School District maintains a Weekly Update Web page where brief, informational material from district staff can be posted. The contents incorporate "must-know" items pertinent to that particular week. Critical links where principals might obtain further information are included. The Weekly Update serves as a clearinghouse where informational bulletins and forms are stored and retrieved for future reference. If correctly maintained and used, the Weekly Update drastically reduces the amount of requests flooding the offices of site administrators.

Another useful tool is a Principal's Resource Binder, which contains sample letters, newsletter articles, planning guides, timelines, checklists, conventional memos, and important policies. Each month principals reinvent the wheel as they draft an array of correspondences to parents, staff, and the community. Such efforts are time-consuming and redundant. All principals face common issues during their careers: mid-year classroom changes, teacher replacements, tragic student or family events, back-to-school and end-of-the year traditions, testing preparation, and employee discipline. Using templates of letters and having examples for such occasions is convenient and saves time.

A Resource Binder delivers practical strategies, solutions, and sample documents for principals to use in the daily management of their schools. With time in short supply, principals need all the help they can get to cross tasks off their lists. Spending fewer hours drafting correspondences provides more time to attend to the pressing matters of learning leadership.

When it comes to communicating and receiving information, people normally fall into one of two categories. To send messages, they either talk or write. To acquire information, they listen or read (McCormack, 2000, p. 210). Once central office staff members determine which style of communication each principal prefers, they can tailor systems and resources to meet each principal's needs. Simplifying the e-chase, reducing perilous paperwork, and managing the information flow allows principals to maintain an acute focus as they go about their daily routines. Facts and directives are best absorbed in small doses.

Relationships, Relationships, Relationships

People are the heart and soul of any organization. To achieve distinction as an excellent employer, central office staff members have to develop and manage good relationships one principal at a time. Holding to promises, maintaining integrity, and spending time together carries tremendous weight in the retention quotient. The alliances a principal forms with supervisors as well as colleagues will maximize the return on a district's investment tenfold. Having a best friend at work, for example, helps principals define who they are and what they can become. The fabric of our lives is based upon the people in it and the desire to do things for those who mean something to us. Camaraderie and belonging form a powerful combination.

In most school districts, the superintendent and senior managers tend to spend time with principals in large groups. This primarily occurs in meetings where information is channeled one way. Unfortunately, such gatherings can create an atmosphere of distance and aloofness. Complicating matters is the fact that many superintendents worry that, if they become too close to their principals, it will diminish respect or breed contempt. What if they need to discipline or terminate the principal, for instance? Conversely, principals are reluctant to share too much about themselves with their superintendent for fear their weaknesses will be revealed and used against them.

To solidify relationships, superintendents and other key district leaders have to make the effort to get to know each principal personally and professionally. The most desirable results occur when this takes place on the principal's turf. If the expectation is for principals to be in the classroom, central office administrators should spend time in the schools. The same due diligence applied to meeting attendance should be used when planning site visits. The strongest relationships are developed through the home field advantage, a single commitment at a time.

English author Charles Lamb once described a conversation he had with an acquaintance as they strolled down the street (Clifton & Nelson, 1992, p. 137):

> Friend: I don't like that man.
> Charles: You don't know that man.
> Friend: That's why I don't like him!

The less we know about people, the less we have in common. This makes it easier not to care about them, which is a dangerous road in any enterprise. When students don't like their teacher, for instance, they develop resistance to learning. The same rings true when employees don't like their boss or believe their boss doesn't like them. If superintendents and principals like one another, they are more apt to work side by side to achieve greatness together. Finding out about a principal's family, outside interests, hobbies, future goals, and life's anecdotes is a true sign of caring.

Building relationships with principals is not a "spectator sport" (Clifton & Nelson, 1992, p. 142). Superintendents have to activate interaction instead of waiting passively for it to occur. But not all principals should be treated the same either. The best superintendents reject the Golden Rule of treating each principal "as you would like to be treated" because people don't all "breathe the same psychological oxygen" (Buckingham & Coffman, 1999, p. 152). Relationships should be built based upon principals' unique strengths, style, and preferences. The implication is "management by exception" rather than by rule. To be truly fair, superintendents have to respond to principals as individuals. Knowing more about the principals under their watch is mutually enriching. Positive relationships bring out the best in principals and make them want to stay with a district.

Make a Principal's Day

If people are a school district's greatest asset, then acknowledgment for what they do is vital to their motivation and happiness. Recent Gallup studies describe praise and recognition as essential components in identifying the most desirable places to work (Boswell, 2003). *Fortune* magazine has noted that the "100 best companies to work for in America" are leaders in their own right when it comes to endorsing the contributions of employees to their company's success (Boswell, 2003, p.1). Whether it's a simple pat on the back or a big brass band, personal accolades carry tremendous weight in satisfying and retaining principals.

In many school systems, if recognition is given to principals at all, it is usually done behind closed doors or through the placement of a letter of commendation in a confidential personnel file. Avoiding the appearance of favoritism is an ingrained practice of public educators. None of us want to make our colleagues feel slighted. Finding the right balance between formal and informal recognition is a wonderful way to make a principal's day. Successful strategies rely on the involvement of senior management as well as the school board. Appreciation bestowed in front of and by peers is also important. Positive recognition of principals leads to enhanced attitudes toward the organization, greater orientation toward servant leadership, and increased loyalty (Boswell, 2003). Often, the little things make principals committed and proud to be affiliated with their school district.

Superhuman expectations from parents, staff, and the central office make it easy to forget there's a real person inside the principal's suit. Principals not only desire respect for their position, they also yearn to be valued as human beings with a life outside of school. Author Barbara Glanz (2003) describes dozens of things a leader can do to regenerate a spirit of inclusion in the workplace. Showing you CARE, according to Glanz, requires a supervisor to Communicate, Appreciate and Affirm, Respect, and Empathize. I've modified Glanz's ideas to offer 10 simple, yet gratifying ways for superintendents to let principals know they care. Most of these gestures cost next to nothing but are priceless in boosting the overall morale and self-worth of principals.

1. Collect photographs of principals at work and display them on a bulletin board in the central office lobby.
2. Keep a photo album inside the superintendent's office depicting principals who receive recognition and awards from the

state, county, local school board, community, or other agencies.

3. Send each principal a birthday card.

4. Have a "message of the day" waiting to inspire principals when they turn on their computer in the morning.

5. Show a funny "year in review" video to parody the humorous side of events that occurred throughout the school year. Don't be afraid to laugh with others at the district's shortcomings and faux pas.

6. Encourage the associate superintendent and other senior managers to do something special during the day or week of the administrator, such as cooking principals breakfast, bringing them ice cream, or taking them to lunch.

7. Have a spring family picnic for administrators. Pay for it out of your own pocket or share the cost with members of the school board.

8. Send a personal note after a principal encounters a difficult situation or decision. This shows empathy and understanding. Do the same when something wonderful happens, as well.

9. Start meetings by sharing positive anecdotes about one or two principals. Acknowledgment should come from the superintendent as well as from peers.

10. Don't be a stranger. Visit and call principals regularly, not just when there's something wrong. Remember, the little things often mean the most.

The demanding parameters of the principalship can make it seem like a thankless job. It's imperative, then, for the superintendent and district leaders to home in on ways to breathe life and hope into their principals. Common sense tells us that happy principals who feel good about their contributions activate favorable results. Because relationships hold more power than official roles and titles, a network of caring within the different ranks of leadership creates a harmonious and loyal administrative team. Take care of your principals and they will take care of you. Go ahead. Make a principal's day!

Refuel the Engines with a Retreat

The revival of principals, even when you get them away from their offices, is not always easy. Listen to how an assistant superintendent describes his district's annual retreat. "It featured some fun, some golf and some interesting speakers from time to time, but the true learning and impact for the district was gone by the time the administrators had traveled the first 100 miles back home" (Malandro & Weiss, 1999, p. 20).

Although this story may possess a familiar ring for some of you who have participated in such a yearly ritual, don't be discouraged. With careful planning and foresight, an annual retreat can be an uplifting experience. Look at how sales soar after a Mary Kay conference. As both contributors and participants, principals will leave a retreat feeling exhilarated and rejuvenated if the experience is meaningful as well as enjoyable. By conducting business in a relaxed atmosphere where cell phones, e-mail, and other interruptions are absent, district leaders can concentrate on their interactions and truly listen to what others have to say.

Whether at the beginning, middle, or end of a school year, a retreat's purpose should be to reflect on district progress, celebrate successes, and prioritize future goals. The idea is to rekindle a spirit of value and worth among principals in a fraternal learning climate. To accomplish this, a committee of principals and key central office staff should work directly with the superintendent to map out an event plan based on participant feedback and district growth targets. If school districts are in the business of learning, the focus of the retreat has to be achievement centered. The context for dialogue and discovery can be framed around storytelling, collaborative exercises, and joint planning sessions. When principals work in high-performance teams, solving problems, dealing with change, and building long-lasting relationships become easier.

Much has been said and written about the importance of growing a strong culture in a school district. "The way we do things around here" embodies the underpinnings of every organization. Setting aside time at a retreat to link the past with the present is important. Too often districts minimize or ignore how events from 10 years ago might still be affecting their principals. Revisiting the history of a particular era can be cathartic and enlightening.

In the book *Shaping School Culture,* Deal and Peterson (1999) describe an exercise used by the West Palm Beach School District at its retreat. To explore the district's cultural roots, administrators were assigned to teams according to the decade they were hired. Groups were instructed to use any medium they wanted to depict the trials and tribulations of that period. Whether they were "old-timers" or "newbies," everyone experienced a common understanding of the history of the district. The superintendent was then able to unfold her vision for the upcoming school year, which paid homage to the past while forging a clear path to the exciting times ahead (Deal & Peterson, 1999, p. 48).

A similar activity took place in Beaverton, Oregon. Using artifacts such as pictures, newspaper clippings, yearbooks, and other mementos, administrators reconstructed the events of a given decade through drawings, poems, skits, and songs. The result was the revelation of how traditions had shaped the district's values and beliefs (Deal & Peterson, 1999, p. 49). When the superintendent surfaces and celebrates the past with principals, it creates a bridge for the future and nudges the administrative culture in a positive direction. A fragile or toxic district culture is a major deterrent in finding and retaining high-quality leaders.

Summertime or weekends are the best times to stage a retreat. Most principals won't object to being away from home if it brings meaning to their work life. For sustained cohesion to exist among principals and senior managers, time for collective inquiry and reflection must be set aside. Simply inviting principals to "go forth and collaborate" will not work. Instead, central office leaders have to provide a venue and process whereby important elements of a principal's craft can be pondered. A retreat gives principals the chance to refuel their engines. The opportunity to bond with peers in this heightened learning structure is something principals will look forward to.

Dancing to the Music

Principals are under tremendous pressure to raise achievement here and now, while advancing the long-term vision and goals of their school and district. It makes little sense, however, for principals to commit their lives to improvement if there is never an opportunity to dance to the music. Celebrations, ceremonies, and awards define a great place to work. Finding things to cheer about creates a zestful atmosphere that evokes happy and healthy principals and helps attract newcomers into the mix.

Celebrations fuel momentum by honoring and thanking people for their contributions. As a public agency, school districts certainly don't have the means to provide extravagant bonuses, trips, or profit sharing for their principals. But, there's no limit to thinking big about awards and celebrations, even when your budget is small. What matters is that the applause is sincere. If it's not, principals see right through it, and celebratory events will be viewed as manipulative flattery rather than genuine appreciation.

For celebrations to have the greatest impact on principals, they should be linked to what is important to the district's success and must derive from measurable gains. The business world relies on four criteria to determine when work deserves to be celebrated. These criteria cross over nicely to school settings and can easily be used by superintendents to invite principals to dance to the music (Clifton & Nelson, 1992).

Quantity Comparisons: Quantity data compares month-to-month, quarter-to-quarter, or year-to-year achievements. Districts can use national, state, or local assessments to establish benchmarks for schools to reach over time. The benchmarks must take into consideration the school's current performance. A quantity goal, for example, might be to increase the number of students taking advancement placement courses or decrease the percentage of students in remedial classes. Narrowing the focus to a specific subject area such as reading, writing, or math is another option. This allows principals and teachers to concentrate on a single mark.

Rated Comparisons: Teacher, parent, and student feedback provide great insight about school climate and the relationship people have with their principal. Awards and celebrations might be tailored around the "Best Place to Work" or "Highest Customer Satisfaction" concepts. Surveys tied to 360-degree feedback can be used to gather this rated data.

Ranked Comparisons: From books, to records, to wealthy people, there is a Top 10 or Top 100 list for just about everything these days. Many states are already well down the path of ranking their schools. The No Child Left Behind Act will soon force all schools in the nation to be ranked whether they like it or not. Accountability in public education is here to stay, so district leaders need to do what they can to help principals get used to it. If achievement rankings seem too heavy-handed, consider using averages to rank highest daily student attendance, highest teacher attendance, lowest number of suspensions, best safety record, greatest parent involvement, or fewest maintenance requests. Similar demographics or building comparisons can be matched to ensure certain schools are not at a disadvantage.

Targeted Comparisons: This type of measurement is cut-and-dried. Either something is achieved or it isn't. The school plan is completed on time or it's not. The school made its Average Yearly Progress or it didn't. Students are proficient or they aren't. The budget is balanced or it isn't. Targeted comparisons are more appropriate when percentages are too complicated to use or when such numerical data cause an uneven playing field.

Some might argue that designing principal celebrations around school comparisons is unfair and elitist. Could individual awards foster a competitive atmosphere that prevents principals from sharing their ideas? What about demographic inequities and standardized testing flaws? Are the comparisons apples-to-apples or apples-to-oranges? Even superstar principals are sometimes uncomfortable with the notion of being singled out in front of their peers, for fear it will cause jealousy and animosity. Teachers' unions who support tenure, vehemently oppose merit pay, and believe that seniority, not performance, should prevail use these same arguments. This philosophy is ingrained in the minds of many principals because most came up through the ranks as teachers. Preserving individuals' self-esteem has always held sway over motivating high achievers who already feel good about themselves.

Experts devoted to the study of leadership say these concerns are unfounded, especially if senior managers make certain that the failure to reach an objective or standard isn't used against a principal (Peters & Austin, 1985). The punishment for not attaining a goal is simply that a principal does not receive accolades. After a while, people tire of being overlooked. Celebrations that revolve around core values and are tied to specific performance standards instill courage in principals. And an extra spoonful of courage can help them overcome anxiety and endure setbacks. Tasting the sweetness of success via individual and team celebrations sends the message that we're all in this together. A collegial spirit is actually built rather than destroyed as people get caught up in the excitement of others. Reticent principals soon learn that their turn will come if they work hard and aim for the target. And as we are reminded by Eleanor Roosevelt, "No one can make you feel inferior without your consent" (Blaydes, 1998, p. 4).

If celebrations are planned with merit and conviction, the sky is the limit, say the authors of *A Passion for Excellence*. "People will work 18 hours a day for months for a T-shirt if the context is meaningful and the presenter is sincere" (Peters & Austin, 1985, p. 306). To celebrate the work of principals, the associate superintendent should plan a Leadership Happy Hour. These social gatherings might occur two to three times a year in lieu of regular meetings and can be held in a principal's home or local establishment, rather than on school grounds. The purpose of a Leadership Happy Hour is to celebrate milestones, support teambuilding, and applaud progress.

Fabulous Bragging Sessions are another strategy to try with your principals (Kouzes & Posner, 1987). Although attendance at these quarterly sessions is voluntary, everyone who participates receives a frameable award signed by the superintendent. Brief, five-minute bragging rights are given to each principal. Stories about a recent improvement or an innovative program that has raised achievement becomes the cause for applause. Attendees are acknowledged for their progress and leave the brag session with a host of ideas to take back to their school sites.

How about some added excitement when principals least expect it? Think about the reaction of principals when the superintendent walks into a meeting dressed in holiday attire? In March, he might come as a leprechaun to recognize four or five principals for something magical they have recently done. Donning reindeer ears and a red nose in December, hoopla might be made about principals who have modeled the ISLLC standards and guided their teachers in delivering the gift of quality instruction. Your most macho, your most sophisticated, and your most timid principals will eventually get caught up in the hoopla!

When a more refined approach is in order, consider a special ceremony to celebrate the loyalty and dedication of principals. One avenue for this is through career service awards. The Edmonton Public Schools in Canada are a good example. Rather than waiting until a principal has been with their district for an eternity or is about to retire, Edmonton acknowledges the continuous service of its employees early in their careers. After one year with the district, a pewter pin is given. At five years, a letter of special recognition is delivered from the superintendent. Ten years of service brings a letter from the board chair, and a sterling pin is awarded at a special function celebrating a principal's 15-year anniversary. Upon the completion of 25 years of service, principals receive a prized memento book at an annual reception honoring long-term employees. Finally, a gold pin is presented at year 30, followed by another personalized memento album upon retirement. The message in Edmonton is that longevity and employee loyalty count for something. Principals see that their time and service to the district is significant and appreciated (Edmonton Public Schools, 2003).

The causes for applause in a school district are endless. But for applause to increase holding power, it should derive from clearly defined goals and provide principals a positive sense of direction. Despite initial awkwardness and trepidation on the part of both the applause givers and receivers, administrators will become more accustomed to these events as they are embedded into the organizational culture. Encouraging principals to celebrate and dance to the music is an excellent way to keep the good ones with you.

Getting Through the "Leaving Moments"

All people face a point in their careers when they have "leaving moments." Another district seems more desirable or less demanding, growth opportunities appear better elsewhere, or an acquaintance from a neighboring district is encouraging you to come to work there. The caliber of the relationships a principal has with colleagues and supervisors is paramount in getting them through these leaving moments. If relationships are poor or nonexistent, principals will leave. When principals are left to fend for themselves or their needs are ignored, turnover is high. The absence of a caring and celebratory climate makes it much easier for good principals to walk out the door and take their experience and talent with them. After all, who wants to work for a school district that excels in mediocrity?

If you think it takes expensive consultants, years of data collection, or a convoluted strategic plan to become a great place to work, think again. You might recall the famous Hawthorne Studies in the 1920s when efficiency experts at the Western Electric Plant in Hawthorne, Illinois, decided to examine the effects of lighting on productivity (Townley, et al., 1999). Because the study occurred during the time Frederick Taylor's principles were widely practiced, the focus was simply to find the right mix of physical conditions, working hours, and job methods to get employees to produce more. However, the researchers became baffled when productivity not only went up for the test group, but improvements were noted in the control group as well.

In the mid-1930s, Professor Elton Mayo of Harvard's Graduate School of Business was called in to expand the research. Mayo and his team began their experiments with a group of women who assembled telephone relays. For a year and a half, they enhanced the work environment by implementing scheduled rest periods, introducing company lunches, and shortening the workweek. The results were so exceptional that the researchers decided to take everything away from the women. The radical change was expected to have a negative impact on productivity, but it didn't. Instead, output jumped to an all time high.

Confused by this development, Mayo questioned the women. He found that the answer wasn't in the production component at all. It was the relational aspect that bore the most influence. The women were receiving so much attention that they no longer saw themselves as isolated and insignificant. Instead, they felt like an integral part of a cohesive team. They also experienced a huge sense of achievement because management was implementing many of their suggestions. Encouraged by this remarkable information, the researchers went on to interview more than 20,000 employees from various plant locations and departments. Workers loved the interviews and, as a result, the company's output soared. Mayo's work led to wholesale changes within the operational structure of industry across the United States.

The Hawthorne Studies provided concrete evidence that for an organization to survive, its management had to pay attention to the people in it. Mayo's findings still carry tremendous influence today as supervisors pursue strategies to involve employees in planning, organizing, and controlling their own work. Because interpersonal relationships and acknowledgment from superiors and colleagues significantly influences the job performance of principals, the superintendent and school board need to lay the foundation for building an enduring workplace. As school districts search for ways to keep their principals, conventional wisdom tells us that the needs of principals and the needs of the organization must converge. To get principals beyond those leaving moments, consider these retention tips:

1. Select principals based upon talent, not just experience and determination.
2. Set expectations that define the right outcomes, not the steps for getting there.
3. Motivate principals by focusing on strengths, not pressuring them to overcome weaknesses.

4. Develop leaders to find the right fit for the principalship; don't just promote people because it's the next rung on their career ladder or they are owed a favor. (Buckingham & Coffman, 1999, p. 67)

Now that you know what separates a good school district from a great one, it's time to let your principals know how much you care. Send them a personal invitation to stay by becoming the district of choice in your city or region. Holding on to good leaders is much less challenging when the internal conditions tender plenty of reasons to remain. Otherwise, principals will concoct a laundry list of excuses to leave. Do your homework. Study the retention practices of other successful school districts to find out how they are filling and supporting their leadership pipeline. Create safety nets to catch principals when they fall. And, most important, be forgiving. Being a principal is a tough job, and if districts are not careful, there won't be anyone left to do it.

7 Planning for the Future

Greatness is not where we stand, but in what direction we are moving.

—*Oliver Wendell Holmes (Bridges, 1991)*

The writing is on the wall. The shortage of school administrators, especially for the principalship, is reaching epic proportions in many parts of the country. Our students and teachers will bear the brunt of the leadership deficit unless we act promptly with a plan. "The effort to identify tomorrow's principals cannot wait until tomorrow—the shortfall is today" (Quinn, 2002, p. 24).

What is the best way for your school district to prepare for the future? First, the important work of principals has to be understood and valued throughout the organization. This means the school board and the superintendent must establish a shared vision regarding administrative development and support. Second, senior managers have to do their homework and assess the current standings of the district's leadership pipeline. Once strengths and gaps are noted, priorities for taking action should be established.

Third, district leaders need to broaden public awareness of the problem. Because most people have only minimal understanding of the crucial role principals and coadministrators play in the success of our schools, spreading the word is tantamount to filling vacancies. Parents, government officials, business leaders, and the community need to know that good schools cannot exist without good principals. Even those without school-age children have a vested interest in keeping the profession alive. High-quality schools help sustain property values, have a favorable economic effect on local businesses, build community pride, and serve as a focal point in neighborhoods. Securing effective principals who can orchestrate the important work yet to be done in our schools is everyone's responsibility and concern.

Don't Be Caught Riding a Dead Horse

Our public schools are losing ground in the battle to find and keep quality leaders. The chasm between supply and demand continues to widen as replacement systems remain "haphazard and serendipitous" (Quinn, 2002, p. 24). A 2001 poll conducted by the Principals' Center at Harvard University found a strategy of "nothing" topped the list of things districts are doing to combat the problem. Although 20 percent of responding districts indicated they are using a "mentoring" or "leadership academy" approach, only 10 percent said they are collaborating with local universities to address shortages (Quinn, 2002, p. 24). Most school districts appear to be suffering from inertia when it comes to harvesting quality applicants, supporting beginning principals, helping leaders grow, and holding on to good talent. To begin the task of preparing future principals, school districts must undertake immediate yet prudent planning.

Although a sense of urgency drives finding solutions to the administrator shortage, caution should not be thrown completely to the wind. If it is, your district might end up with a plan that is poorly communicated and impossible to implement. Sometimes "faster is slower" and "small is big" because all natural systems have an optimal rate of expansion (Senge, 1990, p. 62). The little, finely tuned actions will likely produce the greatest results during the ensuing years. Consider this story as a case in point:

> Years ago a tractor-trailer truck got stuck while heading into a Boston tunnel. City officials were confounded as to how they were going to

remove it. Some suggested they hire a blasting crew to remove part of the tunnel; others suggested that the roof of the truck and trailer be sawed off. Meanwhile, traffic was piling up and patience was wearing thin. Finally, a child stepped forward and suggested they let some air out of the truck tires and back it out to a nearby exit ramp. Needless to say, it worked—the truck was removed and traffic was soon flowing smoothly. (Grant & Forsten, 1999, p. 1)

So what does this tale have to do with staffing the principalship? School systems tend to look for the glass slipper from handsome princes and outsiders, especially when pressure increases and time is in short supply. The best solutions, however, will come from within. To design a leadership development model that rescues your district from the throes of a principal shortfall, try applying these three simple rules: (1) use common sense, (2) start with what exists, and (3) be realistic about what you can and cannot do. The needs in Peoria may not be the same as the needs in San Juan Capistrano.

Nonstop changes, shifting priorities, and an overcrowded agenda have left educators churning through wave after wave of reform. In their search for stability, school districts often become misguided. Even when there is no hope for success, some continue to ride dead horses. With stubborn determination, a few go so far as developing a Dead Horse Riding Plan. Elements of this plan include

- Buying a bigger whip.
- Doing a study to see if lighter riders would improve the dead horse's performance.
- Creating a mission statement that proclaims: "Riding Dead Horses. We're No. 1!"
- Arranging to visit other districts to see how they ride dead horses.
- Harnessing several dead horses together for increased speed.
- Hiring a consultant to revive the dead horse or find a better use for it.

- Blaming the farm on which the horse was born.
- Declaring the horse is better, faster, and cheaper dead.
- Reclassifying the horse as "living impaired." (Tech Solutions, 2003)

There's only one real answer if you discover you're riding a dead horse: Dismount immediately!

The Easy Way Out May Lead Right Back In

In *The Fifth Discipline*, Peter Senge (1990) describes several universal truths about becoming a learning community. As school districts devise a homegrown approach to scaffolding leaders, a few laws described in his book are certainly worth obeying. First, districts must be aware that the cure isn't always better than the disease. Sometimes it's worse. For instance, placing program specialists in schools to cover IEP meetings without a specific communication plan to keep principals in the loop could backfire. If the principal isn't aware of services that are agreed to, a disastrous due-process hearing might result.

Another example involves the establishment of a university partnership. Without a responsible district liaison to recruit participants and represent internal interests, a philosophical disconnect between the two institutions could arise. While the university is proceeding with a strictly theoretical curriculum, the district may be advocating that their future leaders receive heavy doses of reality training. A great divide in district and university ideologies leaves your principals-to-be experiencing the conflict.

These two scenarios are just the tip of the iceberg of what can go wrong if a district looks for the easy way out without thinking things through. As you set sail on your own leadership development journey, it's important that problems aren't inadvertently shifted from one part of the school system to another.

Instead of searching for the easy way out, how about starting where the smallest changes can produce the greatest good? If attrition among your administrative ranks is high, think about working on the relationship-and-recognition aspect of the leadership network. After all, filling the applicant pool without patching the hole in the bucket means water will continue to leak out. Depending upon the size of the hole, the outgo might occur at an equal, if not greater rate than the incoming stream. Another relatively small change that could bring positive results has to do with the number of licensed assistant principals in your pipeline. If you have an adequate number of licensed assistant principals, but they lack the confidence and experience to tackle the principalship, consider starting a Leadership Enhancement and Administrative Development (LEAD) Academy. Veteran principals who keenly understand the fundamental elements of school administration can serve as instructors. Incorporating case studies and field exercises into the program offers practical, behind-the-wheel training to these fledgling principals.

Finally, the superintendent, senior managers, and current principals must avoid becoming prisoners of their own thinking. There might be 101 reasons why a Teaching Assistant Principal program won't work in your district. Try bantering around 10 reasons why it can work. Adding a TAP rung to your career ladder is a low-cost, high-return investment. The key is to provide principals with selection and mentoring guidelines to ensure TAPs are properly nurtured and groomed. Success comes as people move from viewing each leadership scaffold as a single snapshot in time to seeing the entire career ladder as an interconnected whole. In essence, TAPs or assistant principals who have no inclination to expand their horizons hold little value. Filling the reservoir requires principals to look beyond their immediate need of finding an extra pair of hands to the larger purpose of harvesting a potential successor.

Leadership Forecasting:
Preparing Tomorrow's Principals Today

As school districts scramble for solutions to the administrator conundrum, two dichotomies are likely to surface. Picture a group of prospective principals being swept down a fast-moving river as the superintendent and trustees watch helplessly from the muddy banks. In the leadership-disabled district, attempts to save the prospects consist of throwing in life preservers and staff developers. Some prospective principals are strong enough to grab hold, but most float right on by. The leadership-able district, on the other side of the river, sends a team of scouts upstream to see what's causing their people to fall in. As the leaders-in-the-making are pulled safely ashore downstream, the scouts have already begun to install security fences and recontour the landscape upstream. They've also commissioned a special task force to bring back any prospects who were frightened away during the commotion. After all, the leadership-able district realizes that to stay in business and remain competitive, it needs to insulate and cultivate its precious resources.

Regardless of the depth and complexity of the leadership void in your organization, doing nothing is no longer an option. Leadership forecasting, or succession planning as it's called in the private sector, is the only responsible solution. Preparing tomorrow's principals today guarantees continuity for students and teachers, aligns recruitment systems with leadership renewal, engages the superintendent and senior managers in a thorough examination of existing talent, and prevents premature promotions (Hagberg Consulting Group, 2002). After all, who wants to work in a leaderless school?

In simplest terms, leadership forecasting is the proactive development and selection of administrators. The process starts with the end in mind by considering future vacancies, both known and unknown. A viable pool of candidates is waiting in the wings to tackle the principalship and other gateway positions as vacancies occur. It's impossible to predict every opening and need in advance, but forecasting ensures continuity of leadership inside the principal's office, where it counts most.

A coordinated response to the principal shortage compels districts to find and nurture homegrown talent. In the more traditional approach of "replacement planning," districts react to vacancies by filling them with outsiders or insiders who are not necessarily prepared or ready for a promotion. Replacement systems perpetuate the status quo and often lead to performance issues, excessive turnover, unfilled openings over extended periods, and higher external recruitment costs (Hagberg Consulting Group, 2002). Conversely, leadership forecasting is an economical and efficient way to sidestep the experience chasm being caused by the massive retirements on the horizon. When principals retire from the game, a seamless transition ensues as the relief pitcher moves from the bullpen to the mound.

Filling Your Succession Pool

What is the best way to begin leadership forecasting in your district? The first step is to design a mechanism to identify teacher leaders for entry-level assignments. These teachers should demonstrate competency in areas such as instructional knowledge, organization, communication, problem solving, and work ethic. Existing principals have to take personal responsibility for bringing new recruits into the fold. A TAP or TOSA program is an excellent beginning for assembling your succession pool.

The next step is to assess the "promotability" of your administrators. You need to know which assistant principals are most qualified and prepared to assume the role of principal and which TAPs or TOSAs are ready for an assistant principalship. One way to determine promotability is through the use of assessment and development data. Various companies offer services that provide insight to school districts about a candidate's leadership potential, management style, emotional intelligence, and cognitive skills. Another excellent resource is the Gallup Organization. To assist school districts in making fast and accurate hiring decisions, Gallup offers automated telephone prescreeners, an online delivery system, and theme-based interview questions that assess both teacher and principal readiness (Gallup Organization, 2003). Gallup believes that the only way to replicate success is to study it. By studying top performers in hundreds of professions, including the principalship, Gallup has found that effective administrators think, talk, and act differently than their counterparts. To this end, Gallup has identified common talents, or themes, that separate exemplary principals from average ones. Referred to as the Principal Perceiver, interview questions provide a window into a candidate's attitudes and beliefs about working through others to leverage learning. Questions have been developed in 12 key areas:

1. **Commitment:** Principals high in commitment dedicate themselves to the encouragement and development of teachers and students. When commitment is low, principals tend to see their position as a job rather than a mission with a specific purpose of helping others learn.

2. **Ego Drive:** Principals with strong ego drive stake claim to their role as leader and are not afraid to put themselves forth as an example to their peers, subordinates, or students. When ego drive is not evident, principals aren't apt to strive to be their best.

3. **Achiever:** Principals who are achievers have an inner determination that propels them to accomplish things. They have a high energy level. When this theme is underdeveloped, teachers don't view principals as enthusiastic about their work and learning.

4. **Developer:** Those who are developers get satisfaction from facilitating the growth of other people. They know that the more teachers grow, the more likely students will grow.

Principals who lack this skill don't recognize that their success is dependent upon the success of their teachers.

5. **Individualized Perception:** Principals with individualized perception are highly attuned to the individual needs and desires of teachers. They believe that each teacher, like each student, is unique and may require something different. When this talent is absent, principals are more likely to work with teachers and support staff through a "one-size-fits-all" approach.

6. **Relator:** A relator shows care and concern for faculty. Relators make it a point to become close to their employees by getting to know everyone. When the relator theme is weak, teachers are not necessarily cooperative with the principal or each other.

7. **Stimulator:** A stimulator creates positivity, excitement, and good feelings in the school environment. Stimulators instinctively know how to make people feel good. When a principal isn't able to motivate teachers, the climate may be orderly within the school but it won't be enthusiastic or fun.

8. **Team:** Principals high in the team theme have the capacity to get people to work together to achieve goals. Because they extend support to everyone, staff members want to reciprocate and will go out of their way to be cooperative. When this theme is weak, people at the school work as individuals and in isolated units.

9. **Arranger:** Principals who are arrangers are exceptional coaches who keep changing their plays to achieve the objective and win the game. They know how to create systems so that employees are successful. They are described as "always knowing what's going on." Principals who lack this talent tend to organize through rules and schedules that are rigid and inflexible. They are often out of touch with what's happening in the building.

10. **Command:** Principals with a strong command talent have the courage to take action and are viewed as instructional leaders. They are persuasive if necessary and keep the staff focused on helping students learn. When this talent is not in evidence, principals often procrastinate, avoid problems, and sidestep confrontation.

11. **Discipline:** Disciplined principals structure their own lives as well as the lives of others. They are on time, keep their word, maintain good records, use data, and know where things are. When discipline is lacking, principals tend to run the school in an unstructured and lackadaisical manner. This behavior can be frustrating to teachers and staff.

12. **Concept:** Those who are high in concept are able to describe their management style, set performance objectives, and measure their own progress. Principals low in concept are "see it–do it" people. Although they view themselves as practical leaders, they don't embrace a clear philosophy that helps them know what to do and what not to do. When this theme is weak, principals tend to manage based upon ingrained practices and behavior rather than through proven leadership strategies. (Themes © 1992, 1997 The Gallup Organization. All rights reserved. Reprinted with permission.)

First-rate organizations hire first-rate people. Second-rate organizations hire third-rate people (Ragan, 2003). To fill your succession pool with first-rate people, the top internal candidates for leadership roles have to be ferreted out. Screening instruments such as the Principal Perceiver and other Internet assessments assure that district needs are matched with the talents of prospective successors. These tools allow districts to forecast who is ready to be promoted and who is not.

If it's not feasible for your district to rely on an assessment center or Internet service to measure promotability, internally designed protocols are quite acceptable. The idea is to begin the screening process before an opening actually presents itself. A special invitation can be extended to qualified applicants to participate in preliminary interviews and related exercises. To gauge a prospect's understanding of the principals' role in raising student achievement, consider asking questions that explore the value candidates place on their own learning. For instance, you might ask an interviewee to tell you about a book he has read recently on educational leadership and explain an action taken as a result of reading this book. In addition to the in-person interview, applicants might be provided an exit question to measure on-demand writing skills. Some traditional recruitment plans include a written exercise as an initial screening piece. However, when such an assignment is given in advance, a person's true writing ability is difficult to judge as they might have relied upon others for assistance in composing their response.

Another screening mechanism is a professional portfolio that documents how applicants are supporting student growth in their current assignment. Evidence of action-research work, staff performance evaluations, and use of data to improve instruction is compiled in the portfolio. A diverse panel of district administrators can then review the portfolio to determine the candidate's proclivity toward the principalship or assistant principalship. During this entire preselection period, it's important to concentrate on the whole person, not just individual competencies. The more comprehensive the process, the more likely a district is to hire a quality principal who has the perspective and personality to inspire others.

The Dollars and Sense of Replacement Systems

Most school districts underestimate the ramifications of hiring people who are not the right fit or ready for the challenge of a particular assignment. The collective cost of poor hiring decisions can be devastating for an organization. When teachers or administrators are prematurely promoted or lack the skills to assume a principalship, it's a recipe for disaster. Fallout is usually widespread and includes a number of "disengagement factors," including lower productivity and morale among staff, unhappy parents, a tarnished school reputation, political or legal mistakes that warrant repair by others, and stress and added work for supervisors trying to fix problems (Gallup Organization, 2003). These factors may be difficult to attach a dollar value to, but are no less significant than when compared with encumbrances on a budget report.

School districts that take the time to analyze and improve their selection and recruitment efforts will be shocked to discover the savings that can be realized through leadership forecasting (Bernthal, 2002). Even if your district only hires a few new principals a year, the return on investment (ROI) can be substantial. Using data from my own district, Figure 7.1 illustrates the human and financial toll of replacing a single high school principal. On average, a leadership forecasting approach cuts costs in half as compared with replacement planning.

As educational institutions grapple with the administrator shortage and strive to remain competitive, they must become proficient forecasters. Building a succession pool demands forward thinking, customized planning, and an orientation toward the future. Being proactive isn't just about assessment and selection, either. It also requires the creation of a road map to develop, coach, and mentor people once they are in an administrative assignment. To establish a cadre of talent, leadership forecasting has to be propelled by the superintendent and supported by the board. The Instruction Division should own the plan, while the Human Resource department helps guide it. Leadership forecasting puts school districts in the driver's seat by providing flexibility and time to find tomorrow's principals today.

The Goldilocks Rationale for Lost Leadership

At first blush, becoming a leadership-able school district may seem tumultuous and befuddling. In entrenched systems, change often triggers resistance as people fight to preserve what is familiar and comfortable. Scaffolding leaders calls for a coalition of implementers who can firmly embed an administrative career ladder into the culture. Bypassing or removing institutional roadblocks is imperative to a successful transformation.

A litany of reasons exist about why reforms in education have a limited shelf life. A mismanaged process makes failure a foregone conclusion. Excuses and misunderstandings can be likened to the plight of Goldilocks. With childlike innocence, mistakes are explained through extremes and when confronted, we flee. According to DuFour and Eaker (1998), explanations for failure in schools includes a common subset of rationalizations:

- The concept moved too fast. People were overwhelmed.
- The concept moved too slowly. People became disinterested.
- The concept lacked strong backing from the superintendent. Senior managers were ambivalent.
- The concept was micromanaged by the superintendent. Site level personnel had no buy-in.
- The concept was too broad. Baby steps were needed.
- The concept was too narrow. Plans for implementation should have been more aggressive.
- Success was celebrated too soon. The sense of urgency was lost.
- Success was not recognized. There was no momentum to keep the team going. (DuFour & Eaker, 1998, p. 48)

Whether such dangers are real or perceived, complacency toward lost leadership is unacceptable. If the central office looks at principal development possibilities rather than restraints, positive outcomes

FIGURE 7.1

The Dollars and Sense of Recruiting a High School Principal

Cost	Direct and Indirect Costs: Replacement Planning
$775	Advertising: (statewide publication; brochures; online posting)
$985	Recruitment: (2 recruiters to NASSP Job Fair)
$500	Applicant Screening: (review resumes, answer questions, correspondence, track data, references) 10 hours for administrative assistant @ $25/hour 5 hours for personnel manager @ $50/hour
$1,040	Selection Process: Panel Interviews (10 candidates; full day) Subs for teacher panel members (3 @ $90) Sub for classified representative (1 @ $50) Personnel manager (1 @ $350) High school principal (1 @ $300) Parent representative (no cost) Lunch ($70)
$500	Final interview (5 finalists) Meeting with superintendent or associate superintendent (5 hours @ $100)
$2,000	Two years of training, orientation, and coaching (average $2,000 for new principals)*
$9,000	Lost productivity from vacant position (6-week average @ $300/day)*
$14,800	TOTAL

FIGURE 7.1 (continued)

The Dollars and Sense of Recruiting a High School Principal

Cost	Direct and Indirect Costs: Leadership Forecasting
$0	Advertising: Online job posting; open to internal candidates only
$2,500	Assessment Planning: (6–8 candidates) Principal Perceiver ($2,200 one-time cost for Gallup training and materials) Administration of Perceiver by personnel manager (6 hrs. @ $50/hr.)
$450	Preselection Activities: (3–5 candidates by special invitation; half day) Portfolio review and oral interviews (3 management panelists @ $150)
$200	Final interview (2 finalists) Meeting with superintendent or associate superintendent (2 hrs. @ $100)
$1,000	Two years of training, orientation, and coaching (half the cost; candidate is already familiar with the district)
$3,000	Lost productivity (2-week transition @ $300/day)
$7,150	**TOTAL**

*Based on estimates from Bernthal, P. (2002). *Calculating Return on Investment for Selection*. Development Dimensions International. Available: http://www.ddiworld.com.

are sure to happen. Announcing that administrator recruitment, selection, and retention is a priority by action, not rhetoric, makes your plan believable.

Successful school districts, like successful schools, share universal characteristics and beliefs that cause them to excel. Although these qualities cannot be genetically transferred from district to district, they certainly can be modified and adapted within the confines of existing circumstances. Achievement-oriented districts might be old dogs, but they're always learning new tricks. They position themselves for results by writing SMART goals. They subject their deficiencies to a microscope so mistakes aren't repeated. They stay in shape through ongoing conditioning instead of trying to get fit after endurance is lost. They emphasize the value of collaboration because they know it expands their pool of ideas and solutions. And finally, they assess their efforts on the basis of data, not on the basis of intentions.

Whatever restructuring is necessary to scaffold leaders in your school district, the roles and responsibilities of board members, the superintendent, and key members of the management network have to be spelled out. Starting without knowing who's on first and who's dashing toward second gets no one to third and then home. And without any runs scored, you'll leave the game empty.

The Institute for Educational Leadership (IEL) Task Force reports, *Restructuring District Leadership* (2001) and *Reinventing the Principalship* (2000), outline several questions districts should be asking themselves as they assemble their administrative career ladders. These essential questions are modified around the seven key scaffolds of leadership development and retention outlined in this book. Keep in mind that turmoil and conflict are often followed by cooperation and subtle improvements. The idea is to steer clear of the Goldilocks rationale so that leaders are found, not lost.

Assessing the Shortage

- Are we facing a principal shortage in our district? What do we know to help answer this question?
- What do we know about the longevity of our current principals and the next generation expected to replace them when they retire?
- What reasons do teachers and others give for not pursuing a principalship?
- Do women and minorities in principal positions mirror the representation of women and minorities among our student body? If not, how can we support more representative recruitment practices?

Finding High-Quality Candidates

- Are our administrator recruitment practices sufficient to meet the need for qualified and effective leaders for student learning?
- Do we mostly rely on self-selection to deliver school leaders or do we have a strategy to identify and develop promising principals early in their careers?
- How do current principals and central office staff support recruitment efforts?
- What kind of entry-level opportunities are available for budding leaders? Do we have a grow-our-own program? If so, how successful is it?

Getting Prospects Ready for the Principalship

- Do principals receive high-quality preparation? Is that preparation tied to the daily realities and needs of real schools?
- Do we participate in partnerships with universities or other professional organizations to adequately prepare candidates for the complexities of the job?

- If we have assistant principals, are their experiences and job expectations commensurate with what it takes to be a successful principal?

Supporting a Principal's First Years on the Job

- Do new principals have frequent, plentiful, and meaningful opportunities for peer networking, mentoring, and coaching?
- Is there an induction period for beginning principals? If so, how long is this induction?
- What alternative structures, such as distributed leadership and redefined roles, do we have in place to decrease the vulnerability of first- and second-year principals?

Helping Principals Grow

- How strong is our professional development program for principals? Does the model concentrate on important skill sets that deal with leadership for student learning, community engagement, meaningful goal setting, and results?
- Do we evaluate our principals on a regular basis? Do we use multirater feedback? How do evaluations provide principals with the information they need to grow professionally?
- How do we measure the effectiveness of district leadership in supporting and nurturing veterans?

Keeping Good Leaders With You

- Does the district community recognize the value of the principalship? Is the principal provided the autonomy and authority needed to guarantee success?
- Do we offer sufficient compensation to retain high quality leaders?
- Is our organization a great place to work? Do we support and value our human capital by recognizing, appreciating, and listening to principals?

Where Do We Go From Here?

- Do the board and superintendent see the importance of attracting, retaining, and inspiring employees for leadership positions, especially the principalship?
- How can we promote better public awareness of the value and importance of the principalship?
- How do we compare with relatively successful school systems? What can we learn from them?
- Are we riding any dead horses? What is obstructing our progress in scaffolding an administrative development model in our district? Do we make excuses about why things don't or can't work?

The District Planning Guide for Scaffolding Principals (see Appendix C) will assist your frontline in addressing these essential questions and examining in-house recruitment and retention practices. A fundamental challenge in getting started or moving ahead is to gain consensus on the depth of the shortage in your community. Once you begin to understand the present conditions, plans can be made to scaffold teacher, principal, and district leadership. Take advantage of the resources available in your own neighborhood before searching the outlying areas for solutions that may not be doable. Although promising practices are out there, the answers are likely to be found closer to home.

Epilogue: The Rules of the Game Have Changed

Public education is evolving. Although our predecessors grew up in a system of stability with spurts of change, we face a system of change with spurts of stability. Meeting the expansive needs of the nation's children is a Herculean responsibility. From the president, to the moral majority, to the National Association for the Advancement of Colored People, to Fortune 500 chief executive officers, the topic of schooling is on everyone's mind. Political and social pressures run the gamut from complaints about academic rigor and quality to labor market demands for a more skilled work force, to advancing technologies, and to the increasing popularity of learning alternatives such as vouchers, homeschooling, and the charter movement. Educators are grappling with other problems as well. Random outbreaks of violence, deteriorating facilities, overcrowding, teacher shortages, and unprecedented state budget cuts are the issues of the day. Without a cadre of elite leaders, schools won't be able to meet these challenges. The rules of the game have changed.

Members of the education community have to put any differences aside and embark upon a strategic safari to rebuild the principalship. "Principal as plant manager" is no longer good enough. Although site administrators still need to tend to the store, they must do so much more. Twenty-first-century principals are beacons for student and adult learning. Their position requires that they comprehend academic content and pedagogy, strengthen the instructional practices of teachers, collect and analyze data, rally a broad constituency around the single objective of raising student achievement, and deal with the social and political pressures of competing factions.

With the spotlight on the principal, it's time for state policymakers, superintendents, school boards, and senior managers to take a quantum leap. Support and attention has to come from the highest places. If it doesn't, even our superheroes will be hard-pressed to meet the demands of the job. Practices that place unnecessary stress on principals must be abandoned. Central offices need to be restructured to eliminate bureaucratic layers that restrict ideas from moving freely up and down the chain. Administrative career ladders should become part of the business of our business. There's no better time than the present to start walking the talk. Every district can become a pillar of excellence if they lead by example, rather than by convoluted mandates. No district should be left behind!

Let educators unite in our quest to impose order in chaos, offer direction to what otherwise seems to be adrift, and provide meaning and coherence to events that appear random (Blaydes, 1998). It's perfectly fine to stray from the beaten track and become a trail-blazer. What's not fine is to stay at home and wait for an invitation to join the party. If we truly believe we were put on this planet to make a difference in the lives of children, what better way to fulfill this legacy than by harvesting the leaders so desperately needed to make our schools the greatest learning places on earth? Some people only dream of success, while others wake up in the morning and set about achieving it.

Appendix A

Suggested Activities for Developing Leaders

The table describes appropriate activities that can be done by TAPs (Teaching Assistant Principals) and APs (Assistant Principals) to help them learn to lead as they relieve the principal of some responsibilities.

ACTIVITIES	TAP	AP	TASK	DATE COMPLETED	COMMENTS
1. Accident Report	X	X	Complete for student and employee		
2. Activities and Events	X		Plan and supervise student activities (contests)		
	X		Coordinate academic competitions (spelling bee, pentathlon, science fair)		
	X		Coordinate special performances and events (Family Math Nights, Reader's Theater, Literary Day)		
		X	Plan school assemblies		
		X	Supervise dances and athletic events (secondary)		
		X	Maintain annual master calendar of events		

APPENDIX A (continued)

ACTIVITIES	TAP	AP	TASK	DATE COMPLETED	COMMENTS
3. Advisory Committee	X	X	Plan and conduct faculty council and team meetings		
4. Budget	X	X	Review district budget with administration		
		X	Review formula for staffing and budget allocations		
	X	X	Develop school-level spending plan		
		X	Manage site categorical budgets		
5. Building Maintenance		X	Complete work orders		
		X	Develop maintenance schedule for custodian		
6. Bulletins to Parents	X	X	Write newsletter articles		
		X	Monitor and update school Web page		
7. Bulletins to Staff	X	X	Send e-mail messages and memos to keep staff apprised of pertinent issues and timely information		
8. Class Placements		X	Assist principal with class placements (elementary)		
		X	Develop the master schedule (secondary)		

APPENDIX A *(continued)*

ACTIVITIES	TAP	AP	TASK	DATE COMPLETED	COMMENTS
9. Community Activities	X	X	Meet with community organizations		
		X	Organize student participation in community events—parades, beach cleanup, special celebrations		
	X	X	Solicit business partnerships		
10. Contract Language		X	Become familiar with employee contracts		
11. Curriculum Development		X	Participate in district committees		
	X		Chair site-curriculum committees		
12. Daycare	X		Review procedures for addressing issues		
13. Disaster Preparedness	X		Review site disaster plan		
	X	X	Establish and review parent reunification procedures		
		X	Coordinate schoolwide disaster preparedness drills		
14. Discipline	X		Become familiar with suspension, expulsion, and Zero Tolerance policies		

APPENDIX A *(continued)*

ACTIVITIES	TAP	AP	TASK	DATE COMPLETED	COMMENTS
Discipline (continued)	X		Review site discipline plan and procedures		
		X	Chair site-discipline committee; develop and revise plan		
		X	Plan student discipline assembly		
	X	X	Conduct discipline conference with student, teacher, and parent		
15. District Office Organization	X		Discuss and review staff responsibilities and job descriptions of district-level administrators		
16. District Forms	X	X	Become familiar with all online forms		
			Complete the following forms:		
	X	X	➤ Employee Requisition		
	X	X	➤ Graphic Arts Ticket		
	X	X	➤ Mileage Reimbursement		
		X	➤ Purchase Requisition		
	X	X	➤ Request to Attend		
		X	➤ Revolving Cash Voucher		
	X	X	➤ Travel Expense Voucher		

APPENDIX A *(continued)*

ACTIVITIES	TAP	AP	TASK	DATE COMPLETED	COMMENTS
17. Facility Use	X		Review Facility Use requirements and procedures		
		X	Approve Facility Use agreements		
18. Faculty Meetings		X	Help prepare agenda; facilitate meetings		
19. Field Trips	X		Review district and school policy with administrator		
20. Fire Drills		X	Conduct inspection with Fire Marshall or District Safety Coordinator		
		X	Organize monthly drills with principal		
21. First Aid	X		Complete first aid course		
		X	Arrange for first aid and CPR training on campus		
22. Fundraising		X	Advise parent & student groups (booster clubs, PTA)		
23. Gifted and Talented Education (GATE)		X	Manage GATE budget		
		X	Participate in program evaluation		

APPENDIX A *(continued)*

ACTIVITIES	TAP	AP	TASK	DATE COMPLETED	COMMENTS
24. Health Services	X		Review health service procedures with principal		
25. Instructional Aides	X	X	Supervise and evaluate with teacher input		
	X		Provide training in classroom management		
26. Keys	X		Review and discuss procedures with office manager		
27. Lesson Plans		X	Review lesson plan requirements with administrator		
28. Library or Media Center	X		Develop schedule		
29. Lost and Found	X		Establish procedures for lost articles		
30. Lost Children	X		Review and discuss procedures with administrator		
31. Lunch Program	X		Devise schedule and supervise		
32. Lunchtime Activities	X	X	Coordinate lunch activities with student supervisors		

APPENDIX A *(continued)*

ACTIVITIES	TAP	AP	TASK	DATE COMPLETED	COMMENTS
33. Equipment Maintenance		X	Develop or revise checkout system for instructional equipment		
		X	Complete purchase requisition for repair or replacement of instructional equipment		
		X	Maintain current technology inventory		
		X	Conduct technology needs assessment		
	X		Review responsibilities of purchasing department		
34. Music Program		X	Work with site music team on schedule and facility issues		
		X	Collaborate with district music coordinator on staffing or scheduling issues		
		X	Attend special evening performances		
35. Open House		X	Coordinate evening activities with principal		
36. Open Enrollment	X		Review district policy with administrator		
		X	Conduct tours and meetings on school visitation day		

APPENDIX A *(continued)*

ACTIVITIES	TAP	AP	TASK	DATE COMPLETED	COMMENTS
37. Orientation: Teachers	X	X	Conduct fall orientation for new staff members		
		X	Develop staff handbook		
	X		Maintain and update staff bulletin board		
38. Orientation: Pupils		X	Plan and coordinate fall registration (secondary)		
	X		Conduct new student orientation assembly		
	X	X	Lead school tours for new families		
		X	Assist principal in facilitating August Meet & Greet		
39. Outside Agencies	X		Become familiar with the role of all outside agencies		
		X	Review child-abuse reporting procedures with staff		
		X	Meet with local law enforcement officials		
		X	Serve on Youth Task Force		

APPENDIX A *(continued)*

ACTIVITIES	TAP	AP	TASK	DATE COMPLETED	COMMENTS
40. Parent Groups		X	Work with unique parent groups (English Language Learners, Gifted and Talented, Title I, Special Education)		
41. Parent Education		X	Plan and coordinate parent training on topical issues		
42. Parent Surveys		X	Help develop parent feedback survey		
	X	X	Analyze parent survey data; develop improvement plan with leadership team		
		X	Work with principal to determine how to share survey information with staff		
43. Parent-Teacher Association (PTA)		X	Act as advisor and staff liaison		
		X	Attend PTA board and general meetings		
44. Parent-Teacher Conferences		X	Prepare entire school conferencing schedule including notices home, sibling lists, and confirmation procedure (elementary)		
45. Parking Lot		X	Create plan for traffic flow		
		X	Establish alternative drop-off and pick-up areas		

APPENDIX A *(continued)*

ACTIVITIES	TAP	AP	TASK	DATE COMPLETED	COMMENTS
Parking lot (continued)		X	Assist with daily parking lot duty		
		X	Distribute parking permits (high schools)		
46. Personnel Recruitment		X	Screen online applications; review personnel files		
	X	X	Schedule and conduct interviews		
		X	Conduct background checks		
		X	Make recommendations to personnel department		
47. Press Releases	X	X	Write press releases for special events and news media		
	X	X	Submit weekly update column to local paper		
48. Professional Organizations	X	X	Join professional organizations		
	X	X	Subscribe to and read professional journals		
49. Psychological Services	X		Review responsibilities of school psychologist		
	X		Discuss with school psychologist referral procedures and options with outside agencies		

APPENDIX A *(continued)*

ACTIVITIES	TAP	AP	TASK	DATE COMPLETED	COMMENTS
50. Release of Pupils During the School Day	X		Review with administrator legal code, board policy, and school procedures		
51. Retention and Promotion	X		Review school procedures and board policy		
		X	Train staff on retention and promotion procedures		
	X	X	Facilitate Student Intervention Team (SIT) meetings		
52. Safety	X		Review state laws regarding administrative responsibility for safety conditions		
	X	X	Attend Standardized Emergency Management Systems (SEMS) training		
	X	X	Give inservice workshops for staff and update students on safety rules and plan		
		X	Chair site safety committee		
		X	Conduct parent information session on school safety and emergency management plans		

APPENDIX A *(continued)*

ACTIVITIES	TAP	AP	TASK	DATE COMPLETED	COMMENTS
53. Schedules	X	X	Develop schedules (opening and closing of school, lunches, assemblies, annual school activities, staff duties, testing, and parent conferences)		
54. School Assemblies		X	Organize school assemblies and special performances		
55. School Improvement Program		X	Conduct needs assessment		
		X	Serve on committee to help write school plan		
56. Site-Based Management	X		Review current literature and research		
	X		Review role of District Restructuring Council		
57. Special Education	X		Review school referral process with administrator		
	X		Facilitate the student intervention team		
	X		Discuss districtwide special education program offerings with principal		
	X		Become familiar with parent and student rights		
	X		Review 504 process		

APPENDIX A *(continued)*

ACTIVITIES	TAP	AP	TASK	DATE COMPLETED	COMMENTS
Special Education (continued)	X		Review Hughes Bill process		
		X	Lead IEP meetings		
	X	X	Attend special education training		
58. Speech Pathologist	X		Review professional responsibilities of school speech pathologist with school administrator		
	X		Discuss with speech pathologist how testing and referrals are coordinated		
59. Staff Development	X		Review staff development goals in school plan		
	X		Coordinate grade level and departmental staff development		
		X	Plan schoolwide or regional staff development		
60. Student Awards and Recognition		X	Develop school plan for positive incentive program		
61. Student Council and ASB	X	X	Supervise student body elections		
		X	Work with Associated Student Body Advisor (or Activities Director) to coordinate and monitor student-led activities		

APPENDIX A *(continued)*

ACTIVITIES	TAP	AP	TASK	DATE COMPLETED	COMMENTS
62. Student Records	X		Review confidentiality laws		
	X		Review Release of Information requirements		
	X		Review laws and schoolboard policy regarding the content and maintenance of student records		
		X	Provide inservice training for staff on parents' rights to review cumulative information and challenge records		
63. Supervision of Pupils	X	X	Oversee campus proctors or student supervisors		
	X		Provide training in conflict resolution and mediation		
64. Teacher Absence	X	X	Review substitute procedures		
		X	Become familiar with contract language on sick leave, personal necessity, and family health care		
65. Teacher Supervision	X-II	X	Review evaluation criteria with site administrator		
	X-II	X	Become familiar with evaluation timelines		

APPENDIX A *(continued)*

ACTIVITIES	TAP	AP	TASK	DATE COMPLETED	COMMENTS
Teacher Supervision (continued)	X-II	X	Conduct individual performance goal-setting conference with assigned teachers		
	X-II	X	Conduct classroom observations and written summaries		
		X	Write professional improvement plan (PIP) for unsatisfactory performance		
	X-II	X	Complete formal evaluation of assigned teachers		
66. Testing		X	Coordinate state-mandated testing program		
	X		Implement district-level testing program		
	X	X	Interpret school results with administrative team		
		X	Plan teacher training on how to organize and use data		
67. Textbooks	X		Maintain site textbook inventory		
	X		Develop procedures for ordering and distributing books		
	X		Facilitate school textbook pilots		

APPENDIX A *(continued)*

ACTIVITIES	TAP	AP	TASK	DATE COMPLETED	COMMENTS
Textbooks (continued)	X	X	Provide staff training on new adoptions		
68. Truancy and Attendance	X		Review policies with principal and Child Welfare and Attendance office		
		X	Develop incentive program to improve attendance		
		X	Conduct home visits for truant students		
69. Vandalism		X	Complete vandalism report		
		X	Work with custodians to develop anti-vandalism plan		
70. Volunteers	X		Review policies for volunteers on campus		
		X	Conduct training for all volunteers		
		X	Work with office staff to develop sign-in procedures		
	X		Assist with volunteer recognition program		

Developed by Capistrano Unified School District, San Juan Capistrano, California

Appendix B

Planning Worksheet: A Vision for School Improvement

Grade Level and Department _____

	Student Learning and Achievement	Use of Assessments	Curriculum and Instruction	Working as a Collaborative Team
Vision Where do we want to be by the end of the school year?				
Traditions What traditions should we hold onto?				
Transitions What transitions or changes are we moving toward?				

Appendix C

District Planning Guide for Scaffolding Principals

Focus	What's in place now?	What do we need?
Finding high-quality candidates		
Preparing prospects for the principalship		
Supporting a principal's first years on the job		
Helping principals grow		
Keeping good leaders		

References

Alvy, H., & Robbins, P. (1998). *If I only knew—: Successful strategies for navigating the principalship.* Thousand Oaks, CA: Corwin Press.

Archer, J. (2002a, April 17). Principals: So much to do, so little time. *Education Week, 21*(31), 1, 20.

Archer, J. (2002b, May 29). Novice principals put huge strain on NYC schools. *Education Week, 21*(38), 1, 15.

Association of California School Administrators. (2000, June 26). Study confirms principalship shortage in CA. *Ed Cal., 29*(39), p. 1, 9.

Association of Washington School Principals. (2003, June). Membership information. Available: lindat@awsp.org.

Barth, R. S. (1990). *Improving schools from within: Teachers, parents, and principals can make the difference.* San Francisco: Jossey-Bass.

Basom, M. (2002, Dec. 12). Selection, retention and a great place to work. *Educators' Learning Network.* [Online]. Available: http://www.elnetonline.com/research. htm.

Berger, L. (2002, August 4). The rise of the perma-temp. *New York Times,* Education Life, 4A, p. 20.

Bernthal, P. (2002). Calculating return on investment for selection. Development Dimensions International. [Online]. Available: http://wwwddiworld.com.

Blaydes, J. (1998). *The principal's book of inspirational quotes.* Brea, CA: Principal Publications.

Bloom, G. (1999, September/October). Sink or swim no more! *Thrust for Educational Leadership, 29*(1), 14–17.

Bloom, G. (2000). Eleven challenges to a beginning principal's emotional intelligence. [CLASS material, pp. 34–39]. New Teacher Center: University of California, Santa Cruz.

Boser, U. (2002, October 28). Gaming the system, one click at a time. *U.S. News and World Report, 133*(16).

Boswell, G. (2003, June 9). Surveys say . . . "recognition still critical." National Association for Employee Recognition. [Online]. Available: http://www. recognition.org/pages/boswell.asp.

Bridges, W. (1991). *Managing transitions.* Reading, MA: Addison-Wesley.

Buckingham, M., & Coffman, C. (1999). *First, break all the rules.* New York: Simon & Schuster.

Chicago Principals and Administrators Association. (2002, September). LAUNCH program information [Online]. Available: http://www.cpaa.org.

Clifton, D. O., & Nelson, P. (1992). *Soar with your strengths.* New York: Delacorte.

Consortium for Research on Emotional Intelligence in Organizations. (2003). *Emotional intelligence framework.* [Online report]. Available: www.eiconsortim.org.

Copland, M. (2001, March). The myth of the superprincipal. *Phi Delta Kappan, 82*(7), 528–529.

Council of Chief State School Officers. (1996). *Interstate School Leaders Licensure Consortium: Standards for school leaders* [Online report]. Available: http://www.ccsso. org/publications/index.cfm.

Curtis, R. (2002, August). Boston Public Schools. Director of School Development, Boston: MA.

Davis, S. (1998, November/December). Taking aim at effective leadership. *Thrust for Educational Leadership, 28*(2), 6–9.

Deal, T. E., & Peterson, K. D. (1999). *Shaping school culture: The heart of leadership.* San Francisco: Jossey-Bass.

Dell'Angela, T. (2001, April 20). High schools wonder: Who will lead? *Chicago Tribune,* p. DN1.

DuFour, R. (1999, February). Help wanted: Principals who can lead professional learning communities. *NASSP Bulletin, 83*(604), 12–13.

DuFour, R., & Eaker, R. (1998). *Professional learning communities at work: Best practices for enhancing student achievement.* Bloomington, IN: National Educational Service.

Dyer, K. (2001, November). Relational leadership. *School Administrator, 58*(10), 28–30.

Edmonton Public Schools. (2003). Recognition of service. School Board Policy [Online]. Available: http://www.epsb.ca/policy/glb.hp.shtml

Educational Research Service. (1999, February). Study of the principalship. *ERS Bulletin, 26*(6), 1–2.

Educational Research Service. (2000). *The principal, keystone of a high achieving school: Attracting and keeping the leaders we need.* Arlington, VA: Author.

Elmore, R. (1999–2000, Winter). Building a new structure for school leadership. *American Educator,* 6–13, 42–43.

Erickson, J. (2001, November). A rural strategy for filling principalships. *School Administrator, 58*(10), 40.

Fenwick, L., & Collins Pierce, M. (2001, March). The principal shortage: Crisis or opportunity? *Principal Magazine, 80*(4), 25–32.

Forman, D. (1995, March). The use of multimedia technology for training in business and industry. Multimedia Monitor, 30, p. 22–27 [Online]. Available: http://www.sagelearning.com/papers/MMHOM.doc.

Fullan, M. (1997). *What's worth fighting for in the principalship?* New York: Teachers College Press.

Fullan, M. (1998, April). Leadership for the 21st century: Breaking the bonds of dependency. *The Best of Educational Leadership, 55*(7), 15–16.

Gallup Organization. (1992). Principal perceiver. [Online]. Available: http://education.gallup.com/hrd/selcet.

Gallup Organization. (2003). Talent-based hiring. [Online]. Available: http://www.gallup.com/management.

Gemberling, K., Smith, C., & Villenia, J. (2000). The key work of school boards guidebook, National School Boards Association [Online report]. Available: http://www.nsba.org/keywork2/index.cfm.

Glanz, B. (2003, June 9). 25 Low cost, creative ideas to improve morale, enhance productivity, and make your workplace more fun. National Association for Employee Recognition. [Online]. Available: http://www.recognition.org/pages/25ideas.asp.

Goleman, D. (1995). Emotional intelligence. New York: Bantam Books.

Gordon, G. (2003). Do principals make a difference? [Online]. Gallup Organizational Education Division. Available: http://education.Gallup.com/education/review/article.asp.

Grant, J., & Forsten, C. (1999). If you're riding a horse and it dies, get off. New Hampshire: Crystal Springs Books.

Gray, T. (2001, May). Principal internships: Five tips for a successful and rewarding experience. Phi Delta Kappan, 82(9), 663–665.

Grimme, D. (2001). An American crisis: Attracting, retaining and motivating employees. GHR Training Solutions. [Online]. Available: http://www.ghr-training.com/indexarticles.

Hagberg Consulting Group. (2002). Succession planning. [Online]. Available: http://w3.hegnet.com/succesionreplacement.

Hall, N. (1996). Emotional intelligence test. Salum International Resources. [Online]. Available: http://saluminternational.com/emotional_intelligence.htm.

Hargrove, R. A. (1995). Masterful coaching. San Diego: Pfeiffer.

HeartMath Quotes. (2003). [Online]. Available: http://www.heartquotes.net/teamwork-quotes.html.

Helgesen, S. (1990). The female advantage: Women's ways of leadership. New York: Doubleday.

Hersey, P., & Blanchard, K. (1988). Management of organizational behavior. Englewood Cliffs, NJ: Prentice Hall, 1988.

Heylighen, F. (1999, February 19). Change and information overload: Negative effects. Principia Cybernetica Web [Online]. Available: http://pespmc1.vub.ac.be/CHINNEG.html.

Houston, P. (2001, November). Missing in action: The district office. School Administrator, 58(10), 46.

Institute for Educational Leadership. (2000, October). Leadership for student learning: Reinventing the principalship. [Online report]. Washington, DC: author. Available: http://www.iel.org/programs/21st/report.

Institute for Educational Leadership. (2001, February). Leadership for student learning: Restructuring school district leadership. [Online report]. Washington, DC: author. Available: http://www.iel.org/programs/21st/report.

Johnson, J. (2002, May). A public agenda survey: Staying ahead of the game. Educational Leadership, 59(8), 26–30.

Keller, B. (2000, May 3). Building on experience. Education Week, 19(34), 36–40.

Klempen, R., & Richetti, C. (2001, December 12). Greening the next generation of principals. Education Week, 21(15), 34, 36.

Kouzes, J. M., & Posner, B. Z. (1987). *The leadership challenge: How to get extraordinary things done in organizations.* San Francisco: Jossey-Bass.

Lambert, L. (1998). *Building leadership capacity in schools.* Alexandria, VA: Association for Supervision and Curriculum Development.

Le, N. Q. (2003, January 9). E-mail: Heaven or hell? *Orange County Metro.* 29–34.

Lemley, R., Howe, M., & Beers, D. (1997). The new principal: Formulas for success. In *Quality School Leaders* series. Leadership Training Associates in cooperation with National Association of Secondary School Principals, 42–43.

Lovely, S. (2001, November). Leadership scaffolds for an administrative career ladder. *School Administrator, 58*(10), 42–43.

Madison Metropolitan School District. (2002). *Grow your own principal program.* [brochure]. Madison, WI: author.

Malandro, R., & Weiss, L. (1999, November/December). Speedboats on the water of reform. *Thrust for Educational Leadership, 29*(2), 20–21, 37–38.

Manatt, R. (2000, October). Feedback at 360-degrees. *School Administrator, 57*(9), 10–11.

McCormack, M. (2000). *Getting results for dummies.* Foster City, CA: IDG Books Worldwide.

Milliman, J. F., Zawacki, R. F., Norman, C., Powell, L., & Kirksey, J. (1994, November). Companies evaluate employees from all perspectives. *Personnel Journal, 73*(11), 99–103.

Murphy, J. (2001, November). The changing face of school leadership. *School Administrator, 58*(10), 15.

Murphy, J., & Doyle, D. (2001, June). Redesigning the operating environments in school districts and schools. Education Commission of the United States [Online]. Available: http://www.apa.org/monitor/mar98/ smog.html.

Murray, B. (1998, March). Data smog: Newest culprit in brain drain. *APA Monitor, 29*(3), American Psychological Association [Online]. Available: http://www.apa.org/monitor/mar98/smog.html.

National Association of Elementary School Principals. (2001). *Leading learning communities: Standards for what principals should know and be able to do.* Alexandria, VA: author.

New Teacher Center. (2002a). *Challenges facing new principals.* Coaching leaders to attain success (CLASS) training materials. University of California, Santa Cruz: Author. Section 2, 22.

New Teacher Center. (2002b). My life in the last 30 days. *Diary of a 2nd year principal as told to a new administrator program coach.* University of California, Santa Cruz: Author.

O'Laughlin, J. (2001, January/February). Recruitment: A comprehensive approach. *Leadership, 30*(3), ACSA, 14–16.

Olson, L. (1999, March 3). Demand for principals growing, but candidates aren't applying. *Education Week, 18*(25), 1, 20–22.

Orozco, L., & Oliver, R. (2001, July 1). A lack of principals. *Los Angeles Times,* B17.

The people's cyber nation: Great quotes to inspire and motivate you [Online]. Available: http://www.cyber-nation.com/victory/quaotations/subjects/ quotes.html.

Peters, T. J., & Austin, N. (1985). *A passion for excellence: The leadership difference.* New York: Random House.

Peters, T. J., & Waterman, R. H. (1982). *In search of excellence.* New York: Warner Books.

Peterson, K. (1982). Making sense of a principal's work. *The Australian Administrator, 3*(3), 1–4. Deakin University: Victoria, Australia.

Peterson, K. (2001, Winter). The roar of complexity. *Journal of Staff Development, 22*(1), 18–21.

Peterson, K., & Kelley, C. (2001, January/February). Transforming school leadership. *Thrust for Educational Leadership, 30*(3), 8–11.

Pool, C. (1997, May). Conference report: Up with emotional health. *Educational Leadership, 54*(8), 12–14.

Pounder, D. & Merrill, R. (2001, November). Lost luster. *The School Administrator, 58*(10), 18–22.

Quinn, T. (2002, October). Succession planning. *Principal Leadership, 3*(2), 24–28.

Ragan, M. (2003, sample issue). *The Motivational Manager.* Chicago, IL: Lawrence Ragan Communications.

Ruenzel, D. (1998, March). California's school principals: At the center of school improvement efforts. *Ed Source Report, 1*–12.

Sage Learning Systems. (2001). Facts and figures from the worlds of e-learning, training, work, and jobs [Online]. Available: http://www.sagelearning.com/research-papers.htm.

Senge, P. M. (1990). *The fifth discipline: The art and practice of the learning organization.* New York: Doubleday/ Currency.

Sparks, D., & Hirsh, S. (2000, December). *Learning to lead, leading to learn.* National Staff Development Council. 1–16.

Stoddard, S. (2002, December). Things people said: Yogi Berra quotes. RinkWorks. [Online]. Available: http://rinkworks.com.

Stricherz, M. (2001, November 21). School leaders feel overworked, survey finds. *Education Week, 21*(12), 5.

Strong, M., Barret, A., & Bloom, G. (2002, April). *Supporting the new principal: Case studies of intensive principal induction.* Paper presented at the annual meeting of the American Educational Research Association, New Orleans.

Team Builders Plus. (2002, December). 360 degree feedback: A comprehensive 9 step process [Online]. Available: http://www.360-degree feedback.com/360process.htm.

Tech Solutions. (2003, July). The art of dead horse riding [Online]. Available: http:///www.tech-sol.net/humor/one-liner43.htm.

Thomas, D., & Bainbridge, W. (2002, January/February). Sharing the glory. *Leadership Magazine, 31*(5), 12–15.

Townley, A., Schmieder, J., & Wehmeyer, L. (1999). *School personnel administration: A California perspective.* Riverside, CA: Precision Writing.

U.S. Department of Labor, Bureau of Labor Statistics. (2002–03). *Occupational Outlook Handbook.* [Online]. Washington, DC: author. Available: http://www.bls.gov/oco.

University of North Carolina, Charlotte. Department of Educational Leadership (2002, August). [Online]. Available: http://education.uncc.edu.

Wohlstetter, P., & Smith, A. (2000, March). A different approach to systemic reform: Network structures in Los Angeles. *Phi Delta Kappan, 81*(7), 508–515.

Wolfe, P. (1998, July 9). GallupPoll: Employee engagement = Business success. British Columbia Public Service Agency, Government of British Columbia [Online]. Available: http://www.bcpublicservice.ca/awards/aiai_index/emp_engage/gallup.html.

Yerkes, D., & Guaglianone, C. (1998, November/December). Where have all the high school administrators gone? *Educational Leadership, 28*(2), 10–14.

Yukl, G. A. (1998). *Leadership in organizations*. Englewood Cliffs, NJ: Prentice Hall.

Index

Page numbers followed by an *f* indicate reference to a figure.

About the Author

Suzette Lovely has been in public education for 20 years as a classroom teacher, teaching assistant principal, assistant principal, principal, director of elementary operations, and most recently as the chief personnel officer in the Capistrano Unified School District (CUSD) in San Juan Capistrano, California. Lovely attributes her success as a school leader to the endless support and opportunities afforded throughout her scaffolded career in Capistrano.

Lovely developed true empathy for the challenges faced by modern-day principals after sitting in the principal's chair from 1990–1998. During this 8-year tenure, she opened a new elementary school. Under her leadership, both schools where she served as principal were recognized as California distinguished schools.

It is Lovely's quest to support existing principals and cultivate aspiring leaders so that public education sustains its current pipeline of administrators. To maintain a vibrant pool of talent, she provides numerous workshops to seasoned as well as novice school leaders. In 1999, Lovely designed the Capo LEAD Academy around the California leadership standards to offer fieldwork credit to practicing administrators completing their licensure requirements. In addition, she works as an adjunct professor in the master's in education program at Chapman University.

Lovely has presented her insights at several state and national conferences including the Association of Supervision and Curriculum Development (ASCD), the National School Boards Association (NSBA), the California School Boards Association (CSBA), and the National Association of Elementary School Principals (NAESP). In

1999 and 2000, she helped coordinate a principals' symposium for the Orange County Department of Education.

She lives in San Clemente with her husband and two dogs and may be contacted through Capistrano Unified School District, 32972 Calle Perfecto, San Juan Capistrano, CA 92675 USA. E-mail: slovely@capousd.org or sue.lovely@cox.net.